MW01600782

QUANTUM CHRISTIANITY
FAITH AND FACTS

Vol.1 of 7
[Christ Consciousness]

By. A.C Benson

WHO '[I] AM'

I can not imagine living life without my faith, or not having a God or higher power; a Creator who can see the whole picture, outside of space and time. There is no doubt in my mind we have a Creator who is good and gracious. Now, let me not forget to mention that, I was raised on the conservitive baptist side of christianity. It was tough because it is very legalistic, which, in my opinion, is the opposite of what Jesus' teachings were about. But I digress. So there's my faith, table that.

Math and science were always strong subjects for me. I want to say my ah ha moment was my junior year in HS when I took physics class. I still remember my teacher, Mr. Kovalcin, a published professor. His passion for what he taught and the fact that it made sense to me was inspiring and exciting. It was like being able to get a glimpse of God's mind, God's intelligence.

I was also an athlete, basketball player. I was being recruited at universities and was interested in studying athletic training and/or kinesiology for my bachelors. Mr. Kovalcin would give me questions that were sports related. For example,

Phil is trying to dunk a basketball and leaves the ground with a vertical velocity of 3.5 m/s. a. What is Phil's vertical acceleration immediately after takeoff? b. What is the peak height Phil's center of gravity will attain if it started at

1.2m? c. How much time elapses before Phil will reach his peak height?

The fact that I could equate athletics with physics was fascinating to me. Everything could be predetermined in an accurate environment, should enough data be present. Of course, this is called biomechanics and is a part of what I studied. My BS is in Kinesiology. I also was a certified athletic/personal trainer before I started teaching health and phys ed and coaching basketball at a variety of levels.

So here was my dilemma! I KNOW that GOD is real. I've had 'HIM' move in my life so many times, again no doubt we have a Creator. But I also KNOW that physics is REAL [israel] and the earth was created by God in a mathematical way. Thus began my journey to connecting those dots. If we are all created by the same one and only GOD, then all is from GOD and it all has to make sense, somehow, someway.

Romans 8:28 And we know that all things work together for those who love God, to those who are called according to his purpose.

INTRODUCTION; FOREWORD

So: After a lovely year for humanity in 2019/20, I found myself uncovering much truth and understanding of the illusion of, what I thought, was my "reality". At the same time, I began to fully embrace my spirituality (not religion) with my higher self, becoming fully awake and enlightened. In a split second, a 'KNOWING' that transcends all space and time, entered me. It was like a volt of energy traveled from the core of my body up and out into eternity. Simultaneously, the same energy coming back in return to my roots. Fireworks went off in my head. I sensed that I had reached a new and different level of evolution. Something in my brain, in my DNA and in my heart was being ignited, like a spark into a fire. It was my "burning bush" moment. I had to continue to walk on the road God was calling me to walk, in obedience.

QUANTUM CHRISTIANITY: 7 VOLUME SERIES

Book Volume #

CHRIST CONSCIOUSNESS
CHAPTERS

PRAYER/Meditation/Dedication:

To the Infinite and Eternal Creator and Source of Light, Love, Logic and Reason. I pray humanity will awaken to your TRUTH, and see your LIGHT, using [our] mind and hearts, that was/is/and will continue to be transformed in [your] IMAGE.

In Your Mighty Name, Amen

01.

What is Consciousness?

As a kid, the movie pinocchio was always deeper than it needed to be for me. I could never watch the whole thing in its entirety because it just made too much sense, literally. Thus it was frightening and made me feel uneasy. Let's recap shall we.

In 1940, Disney released, (changed from the original italian fabel), their version of a G-rated cartoon about Geppetto, an elderly carpenter (God) who, in his loneliness, decides to craft a wooden child puppet for himself. (man) One night, when the doll was complete, the old man went to bed and saw a star illuminating the night sky (THE LIGHT). It was not just any star, but a Wishing one (divine /miracle/magic).

Since it was rare for a star like this to be seen, he looked through his window, and made a wish: "Star light, star bright, first star I see tonight. I wish I may, I wish I might have the wish I wish tonight (prayer). Figaro, you know what I wish," he asked his kitten, "I wished my little Pinocchio might be a real boy." (a companion) He looked at his doll and sighed,"Wouldn't it be nice," Then a tiny little cricket named Jimmeny, responded saying, "A very lovely thought, but not at all PRACTICAL," (mind/ logic) To make it POSSIBLE, one would need 'DIVINE' power)

Mark 9:23 All things are possible when we believe.

The star was not actually a star but a fairy (angel). She had heard Ghepetto's wish (prayer) and would make his wish come true (blessing). She made Pinocchio a living puppet (man, along with Jiminy by his side, a tiny cricket assigned to act as his conscience (Christ). The puppet must prove to be worthy of becoming a real boy (Evolve to HUman, Higher dimensional man). Throughout all his mischievous acts and experiencing various challenging decisions, he understands how a real boy should behave. Jiminy was guiding his path, asking questions, so he can come up with the answer himself. Hmmm sounds a lot like how Jesus taught, i.e. similar Methodology.

Don't we all have an inner voice telling us what to do or where to go? We have a moral compass, no one in history can conclude otherwise. The question is, why is it that science can not physically prove it exists? Conceptually, it can conclude that [it] is there. If [it] is there, where does [it] go after the body is no longer "alive"? Where does it go in the afterlife, eternal life or rebirth/reincarnation? Are those things even different or are they the same? The story of Pinocchio is HIS journey from being created as a meta-physical being with form, to becoming divinely alive navigating his 'personality' and spirit. By the end, he is able

18

to connect those 2 aspects, to 'find' himself as a REAL boy, his soul. Shall we dive in?

Recently, consciousness has become a significant topic of research, all across academia. It is studied in cognitive science, psychology, linguistics, anthropology, psychology and neuroscience and of course in a variety of 'religious' structures. The primary focus is getting an understanding of what information is metaphysically and celestially present in consciousness. It is determining the mechanics and the "other stuff" that make up [self identity].

The earliest use of the word 'consciousness' or 'conscience' in the English language dates back to around the 1500s. The English word "conscious" originally came from the Latin (con- "together" and scio "to know"). It meant "knowing with" or "having joint or common knowledge with another". Furthermore, WITHscience = CONscience! There were many occurrences in Latin writings of the phrase conscious sibi, which translates literally as "knowing with oneself", "sharing knowledge with oneself about something", or "knowing that one knows". Sounds like an oxymoron to me, a palindrome of sorts. (which means the same from one end as it does from the other)

The definitions of consciousness in Webster's Third New International Dictionary is this:

Awareness or perception of an inward psychological or spiritual fact; intuitively perceived knowledge of something in one's inner self inward awareness of an external object, state, or fact concerned awareness; the state or activity that is characterized by sensation, emotion, volition, or thought; mind in the broadest possible sense; something in nature that is distinguished from the physical the totality in psychology of sensations, perceptions, ideas, attitudes, and feelings of which an individual or a group is aware at any given time or within a particular time span; the part of mental life or psychic content in psychoanalysis that is immediately available to the ego.

The Oxford Living Dictionary defines consciousness as "The state of being aware of and responsive to one's surroundings.", "A person's awareness or perception of something." and "The fact of awareness by the mind of itself and the world."

If we assemble this information together, in a big clay ball of energy, (I like to illustrate), consciousness is [THIS] very second. Where your spirit (spiritual or celestial self/energy), and your body (metaphysical elements), meet/collide/mesh/explode, YOUR SOUL. Each second of everyday; every single moment, we are constantly making a decision on what to do or say next. Something deep down pushes us towards a direction. This "voice" gives us clarity on what would be best, and then act on it. So easily put, Consciousness is being ALIVE. Your consciousness is energy. It is never created or destroyed but can be transformed. This is the Law of Conservation of Energy. In biblical terms ; it always was, is and will be. Hmmm sound familiar yet?

In my opinion, this is what "has eternal life" from a faith perspective. Something about who we are, lives forever.

In every single religion and culture in the world, there is belief in a higher power and an afterlife of some sort. As a human species we can feel that in our very essence of who we are. This is called Cellular Memory. Since everything came from the same source, we are all interconnected (Entanglement Theory). Even with minimal scientific proof the majority of humanity still believes in this unexplainable feeling of mission and purpose. That there is more outside of what we can see in this world. Faith.

The Age of Faith is over, Woohooo! We no longer have to just "believe" . We can KNOW! We are now living in a time where (All that was, is and will be) will meet, Event Horizon (google it). The knowledge, technology and mathematics have evolved to a point where ancient texts can be understood for what they were truly meant to be understood as. THE ETERNAL INFINITE WORD. (book II in this series)

John 1:1 **In the beginning** was the Word, and the **Word was with God**, and the **Word was God**. 2 He was in the beginning with God. 3 All things were made through Him, and without Him nothing was made that was made. 4 In Him was life, and the life was the light of men. 5 And the light shines in the darkness, and the darkness did not comprehend it.

This passage does not equate to the "bible". Although the bible is inspired scripture from God, it most certainly is not the only God inspired text. In fact, NO WHERE in the bible does it say that the BIBLE is God's WORD. How did we mess that one up! Think about when someone says or I write, "google it" . It doesn't necessarily mean, use google . It just means to look it up on the internet. Similarly with , "the Word of God".

Moving on....

Dualism or duality, is an ancient concept that is deeply rooted in Greek thought. However, long before that, the ancient scriptures taught that mankind was made in God's image and that 'Adam' (which is Hebrew for 'man'), needed the spirit breathed into him before becoming a 'living' soul. Almost 2000 years later Plato and Aristotle reasoned that the human mind or soul could not be identified with the physical body (pre quantum physics), Rene Descartes reinforced this concept and gave it a name, dualism.

Descartes' is famous for saying, "cogito ergo sum"(I reflect therefore I am). It is the answer to the Theory of Everything. (we just haven't figured out the mathematical equation yet, or have we?) Descartes said that the immaterial mind and the material body are two completely different types of substances and that they interact with each other. His rationale was that the body could be divided up by removing a leg or arm, but the mind or soul were 'entangled'. One could not exist without the other. In binary, these are the 0's and 1's . The Vessel and the Host; The ring and the sword/wand; The seed and the egg; CREATOR and the CONSUMER. When combined, they ARE the CREATION.

This concept is difficult to accept for someone with a materialist, or evolutionist worldview. But on the contrary, bible believers also have a difficult time with this concept.

22

This is because it accepts both extremes to be true and necessary, in the 'Theory of Everything'. Why can't it be both? Why hasn't this thought of putting 2 concepts together to try and seek the mind of God gone mainstream? Everything is created from the same God Source, Quantum Christianity.

Richard Maurice Bucke, a mystical psychologist and author of the 1901 book, 'Cosmic Consciousness: A Study in the Evolution of the Human Mind', highlights three types of consciousness: (plato and aristotle had similar views and theory)

1.'Simple Consciousness', awareness of the body possessed by many animals.

2.'Self Consciousness', awareness of being aware, possessed only by humans.

3.'Cosmic Consciousness', awareness of the life and order of the universe; which is "a higher form of consciousness than that possessed by the ordinary man.

"HU-MAN= Higher Universal man"~ AC BENSON

Bucke claimed this; consciousness shows that the cosmos is not made up of dead matter floating on the wind of random chaos. It is quite the opposite actually. The cosmos is entirely non-material, almost entirely spiritual but yet entirely 'alive'. He concluded that everyone and everything has eternal life. His theory also suggested that the universe IS God, and that God IS the universe. We are all connected because we all come from the same Source, that Source being GOD. Today this theology has a name, Quantum Physics aka Quantum God. (Google God Particle to follow the rabbit down that hole) This has further been proven in metaphysics where they have concluded that matter only makes up a fraction of the universe. In fact 99.999% of our 'reality' is empty space or unknown.

For me, I personally land in this area of 'THEORY', which is really another word for FAITH. There is a Cosmic GOD and he is ALL Consciousness. I am able to connect my beliefs as a christian, without ignoring the facts of what is scientifically proven. It is about finding the balance between the mind of God and the heart of God. If all is OF GOD, and FROM GOD, then there MUST be scientific theology that makes a connection to everything. (The Law of Everything or the Law of One, google it).

In my opinion, we have a micro and macro consciousness (creator GOD and SELF). We also have a micro and a macro cosmos (THE creation at cellular and interstellar level). We can become our higher universal self or HU-man, once the transition or awareness is activated. Then a being becomes a co-creator and a part of a Collective Christ consciousness, representing the SOUL of God. I like to think of Christ Consciousness as God's spirit fractalized in its smallest binary form; Metaphysically (photons of light); and celestially (with the spirit of unconditional love). GOD is able to tap into us, and us into God. This allows us to make the best decisions based on all aspects of reality, in that specific moment in [time]. Team work makes the dream work! After all we are 'His' disciples; God's hands and feet; the Body of Christ. Each part of the body has a role. Each role is different, but all necessary.

1 Corinthians 12:12-31 - For as the body is one, and hath many members, and all the members of that one body, being many, are one body: so also [is] Christ.

Romans 12:4-5 - For as we have many members in one body, and all members have not the same office:

1 Corinthians 12:27-31 - Now ye are the body of Christ, and members in particular.

Ephesians 4:16 - From whom the whole body fitly joined together and compacted by that which every joint supplieth, according to the effectual working in the measure of every part, maketh increase of the body unto the edifying of itself in love.

Colossians 1:18 - And he is the head of the body, the church: who is the beginning, the firstborn from the dead; that in all [things] he might have the preeminence.

Cosmic consciousness is an interconnected way of seeing things, which is more of an intuitive knowing than it is a factual understanding. It is the perception of the universe and all of endless possibilities, connected and held together with the glue of unconditional LOVE. And what is love? GOD!

1 John 4:8 He that loveth not knoweth not God; for God is love.

1 John 4:16 And we have known and believed the love that God hath to us. God is love; and he that dwelleth in love dwelleth in God, and God in him.

Sounds a little bit like quantum theory to me. 'Something' in the past, present, and future, outside of space and time, is living inside of you. ('google' quantum vacuum, wormholes and black holes)

It is the REVELATION, the climax, ascension, pinnacle, mountain top, nirvana , enlightenment; of religious and spiritual growth of humanity's evolution, it is happening NOW. These are BIG changes, and it's coming FAST! Woohoooo. Truth, Justice, Happiness, harmony coming right up! Humanity will finally understand who and what GOD is and how we can LIVE according to his purpose in peace and harmony.

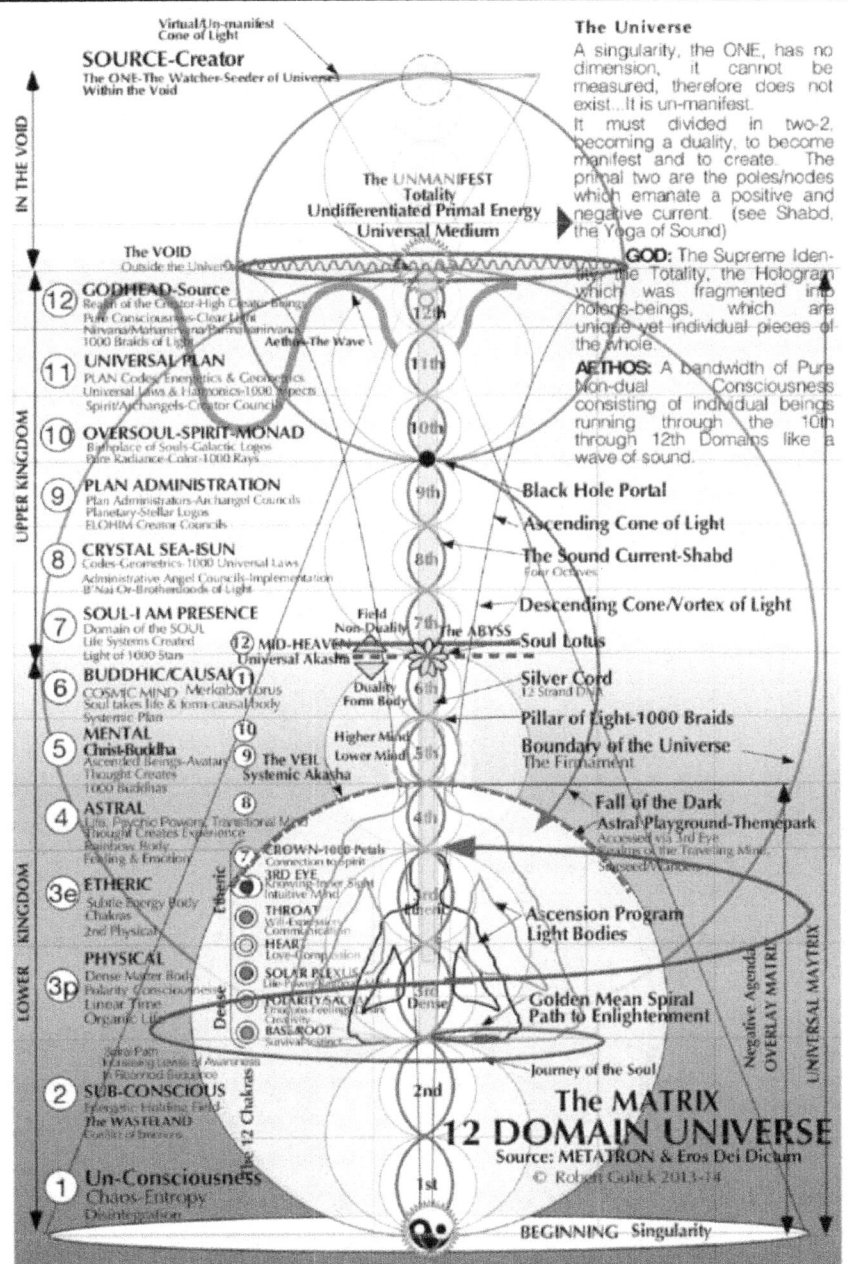

SOURCE-Creator
The ONE-The Watcher-Seeder of Universe
Within the Void

Virtual/Un-manifest
Cone of Light

The UNMANIFEST
Totality
Undifferentiated Primal Energy
Universal Medium

The VOID
Outside the Universe

The Universe

A singularity, the ONE, has no dimension, it cannot be measured, therefore does not exist... It is un-manifest.

It must divided in two-2, becoming a duality, to become manifest and to create. The primal two are the poles/nodes which emanate a positive and negative current. (see Shabd, the Yoga of Sound)

GOD: The Supreme Identity, the Totality, the Hologram which was fragmented into holons-beings, which are unique yet individual pieces of the whole.

AETHOS: A bandwidth of Pure Non-dual Consciousness consisting of individual beings running through the 10th through 12th Domains like a wave of sound.

IN THE VOID

UPPER KINGDOM

LOWER KINGDOM

(12) GODHEAD-Source
Realm of the Creator-High Creator Beings
Pure Consciousness-Clear Light
Nirvana/Mahanirvana/Parinirvana/nirvana
1000 Braids of Light   Aethos-The Wave

(11) UNIVERSAL PLAN
PLAN Codes-Energetics & Geometrics
Universal Laws & Harmonics-1000 Aspects
Spirit/Archangels-Creator Council

(10) OVERSOUL-SPIRIT-MONAD
Birthplace of Souls-Galactic Logos
Pure Radiance-Color-1000 Rays

(9) PLAN ADMINISTRATION
Plan Administrators-Archangel Councils
Planetary-Stellar Logos
ELOHIM Creator Councils

(8) CRYSTAL SEA-ISUN
Codes-Geometrics-1000 Universal Laws
Administrative Angel Councils-Implementation
B'Nai Or-Brotherhoods of Light

(7) SOUL-I AM PRESENCE
Domain of the SOUL
Life Systems Created
Light of 1000 Stars

(6) BUDDHIC/CAUSAL
COSMIC MIND   Merkabba Torus
Soul takes life & form-causal body
Systemic Plan

(5) MENTAL
Christ-Buddha
Ascended Beings-Avatars
Thought Creates
1000 Buddhas

(4) ASTRAL
Life, Psychic Powers, Transitional Mind
Thought Creates Experience
Rainbow Body
Feeling & Emotion

(3e) ETHERIC
Subtle Energy Body
Chakras
2nd Physical

(3p) PHYSICAL
Dense Matter Body
Polarity Consciousness
Linear Time
Organic Life

Astral Path
Traversing Levels of Awareness
& Recorded Existence

(2) SUB-CONSCIOUS
Energetic Holding Field
The WASTELAND
Conflict of Emotions

(1) Un-Consciousness
Chaos-Entropy
Disintegration

Aethos-The Wave

12th

11th

10th

9th

8th

7th Field Non-Duality
Universal Akasha
(12) MID-HEAVEN
The ABYSS

6th Duality
Form Body
(1) Merkaba

5th Higher Mind
Lower Mind
(10)
(9) The VEIL
Systemic Akasha

4th
(8)

(7) CROWN-1000 Petals
Connection to Spirit
3RD EYE
Knowing-Inner Sight
Intuitive Mind
THROAT
Will-Expression
Communication
HEART
Love-Compassion
SOLAR PLEXUS
Will-Power-Balance
POLARITY-SACRAL
Emotion-Feeling-Dark
Creativity
BASE-ROOT
Survival Instinct

3rd

2nd

1st

Black Hole Portal

Ascending Cone of Light

The Sound Current-Shabd
Four Octaves

Descending Cone/Vortex of Light

Soul Lotus

Silver Cord
12 Strand DNA

Pillar of Light-1000 Braids

Boundary of the Universe
The Firmament

Fall of the Dark
Astral Playground-Themepark
Accessed via 3rd Eye
Creations of the Traveling Mind
Stopped/Trapped

Ascension Program
Light Bodies

Golden Mean Spiral
Path to Enlightenment

Journey of the Soul

The MATRIX
12 DOMAIN UNIVERSE
Source: METATRON & Eros Dei Dictum
© Robert Gulick 2013-14

BEGINNING... Singularity

The 12 Chakras
Etheric   Dense

Negative Agenda
OVERLAY MATRIX

UNIVERSAL MAYTRIX

02.

Who or what is the 'Christ'?

The term 'The Christ' originated from the concept of the messiah in Judaism, thus the term judeo/christian. As Christians, we believe that Jesus is the messiah foretold in the Hebrew Bible (Christian Old Testament). These Ancient hebrew scriptures were originally written in aramaic, in the era of time before that of the Major prophets like Isaish.

'CHRIST' is used by us Christians, as both a name and a title, when referring to Jesus. *Now, before I move on, I want to say for the record that in vol 2 of this series, I will be discussing the controversy of the name that became Jesus, and biblically and historically how it came to be. Perhaps you are thinking, 'gee I didn't realize there was a controversy?' Yeah sooo table that and get my next book =)*

Anywho, so "Christ Jesus", means "the Messiah Jesus". The original followers of Jesus usually referred to him as "Jesus of Nazareth" or "Jesus, son of Joseph". Jesus came to be called "Jesus Christ", by later Christians (timeline debated), who believed that his crucifixion and resurrection fulfill the prophecies of the Old Testament. Different areas of academia have several ideas on the timing of it all if you're interested in another rabbit hole.

In the Ancient Greek text of the deuterocanonical books, the term "Christ" (Χριστός, Christós) is found in 2 Maccabees 1:10-20 (referring to the anointed High Priest of Israel), also in the Book of Sirach 46:19-22. It was in relation to Samuel, prophet and teacher of the kingdom under Saul. In pre-New Testament references, at the time of Jesus, there was no single form of Second Temple Judaism. However, for centuries the Jews had used the term moshiach ("anointed") to refer to the coming deliverer or messiah.

The earliest Christian writings gave several titles to Jesus, such as Son of Man, Son of God, Messiah, and Kyrios, which all came from the Hebrew scriptures. These titles come from two concepts. First, that "Jesus is a pre-existent/pre-birth divine entity who becomes human in Mary and then returns to God, his source," and second that "Jesus is the perfect vessel or body that holds the spirit of God." My question again is, why the duality!? Lets reconcile the polarities and create unification of humanity. Is that not the message of Jesus?

In Mark 1:1 it says, "The beginning of the gospel of Jesus Christ, the Son of God". This identifies Jesus as both Christ and the Son of God. In Matthew 1:1 it too uses Christ as a name and in Matthew 1:16 it explains it again saying: "Jesus, who is called Christ" . In Matthew's account, Jesus at first refused a direct reply to the high priest Caiaphas's question: "Are you the Messiah, the Son of God?", where

His answer is given merely as Σὺ εἶπας (Su eipas, "You have said it"). In Luke, Jesus is asked: 'Are you then the Son of God?', to which to his account , Jesus answered: Ὑμεῖς λέγετε ὅτι ἐγώ εἰμι (Hymeis legete hoti ego eimi, "You say that I am". In the Gospel of Mark, when asked 'Are you the Messiah, the Son of the Blessed One?', Jesus tells them: Ἐγώ εἰμι (ego eimi, "I AM").

When Jesus would not deny his 'claim' to divinity, it angered the high priest, thus Jesus was accused of blasphemy and then put to death. Before Pilate, it was the refusal to deny his Divine connection to his Father, God that started his smear campaign. GEEE, so Jesus came to sacrifice his body for the sins of humanity, but instead of 'thank you's', the religious men condemned him. So don't shoot the messenger. I too am here to spread the GOOD NEWS, eternal 'WORD' of God. Christ's energy is the essence of being, that transcends all space and time.

Why do we put a limitation on what God is capable of, to one small miniscule moment in the history of eternity. GOD still inspires divine text and spoken word today. We hear them on Sunday morning from our pastors and in the early morning chirping of the birds singing. We see them in the techno color of the sunset after a fresh rain. We see it in the magic of numbers, in math equations as well as in all the ways we have evolved as a species.

As I personally understand it, CHRIST is a title given to the messiah or savior. Jesus is the perfect representation of Christ Consciousness, THE CHRIST. From here, we would then take into account the roman catholic church (adding paganism), protestantism (rebellion against roman church), puritist, calvinist and so on and so forth, each 'group' understanding the 'Scriptures' differently and to their OWN understanding. The Bible says in Proverbs 3:5-6, Do not lean on your own understanding (man). Acknowledge HIM (the Cosmic Christ Consciousness) in all YOURS ways, and [HE] shall direct YOUR path. This would be a fantastic sermon series! Furtick?

The way I 'entangle' this into Quantum physics is by accepting that ALL is 'right' and 'correct', because it's all necessary in order for God/Universe to continue to grow, expand, and evolve. If humanity is able to connect the dots with metaphysical evidence, and strip away MAN'S PERSONAL UNDERSTANDING of the inspired text of God, we can see the beauty of God expressing himself through us, The Body of Christ.

Christology literally means "the understanding of Christ," the nature (person) and work (role in salvation) of Jesus in Christianity. It is the study of Jesus the Christ's humanity(metaphysical), divinity(celestial), and the relation between the two. From the second to the fifth centuries, defining the term 'Christ', was a major debate in the early church. The Council of Chalcedon in 451 AD issued a formal doctrine which stated that Jesus the CHRIST [was] a perfect union of being human and divine, "united with neither confusion nor division" (reconciliation of polarities). Most of the major branches of Western and Eastern Orthodox Christianity use this doctrine.

For the Sake of consistency in my mapping and blueprinting process, I will use the following philosophy for the basis of my research; CHRIST is both divine and human. Jesus is one of many sons and daughters of GOD. Jesus would constantly remind people to worship the Father, and not him. He made sure that his followers understood that they were in the family of God too (brotherly or Agape love). He got down on his knees and washed their feet; THE CHRIST (GOD in human form). It is BOTH divine and human, BALANCE (You will hear me talk about balance in everything and anything) For every action there is an opposite or opposing reaction. Law of relativity.

In my opinion, the goal of christianity needs to shift to universal unity, respect, and coexistence. We need to establish a frequency and vibration of peace and harmony. There is one GOD, and one Savior (get out of jail free card), because God could see down the road into the 'future' of eternity, of who we are, and what we turned into. He saw that we would destroy ourselves, thus humanity would never see a new heavens and a new earth. So Jesus was sent as a gift of grace (since he could see that we screwed it up so bad). So he would be able to one day only have a heavens and an earth of goodness, love, light and logic and reason. There are two ways to be 'with God' and not 'apart' from him. First way is to accept the free gift of faith through Jesus, surrendering it all. The second is to, " get it" or "be clear". This means to be fully awake, enlightened and ascended to the wisdom of God's mind and the love of God's heart. This does NOT mean to be perfect, as we all ' fall short' of the Glory of God.

Having extreme concepts in anything, creates hostility and negative energy towards that person/ place/ thing. Think about a battery, there is a positive charge and a negative charge, the polarities. The closer to the center to neutral we get, the forces become usable energy. When the charges are 'opposing' or far apart, they have no 'power'. One can not exist without the other. This happens at the conscious and subconscious levels of our mind and hearts as well. Once that energy is stuck, trapped and cant move or flow, the body reacts. It is no longer at "ease", it is with dis-"ease". We have discomfort because the vibration and frequency of the energy is not in harmony. If we all could just chill out and embrace the Age of Aquarius.

Luke 22: 7 Then came the Day of Unleavened Bread, when the Passover must be killed. 8 And He sent Peter and John, saying, "Go and prepare the Passover for us, that we may eat." 9 So they said to Him, "Where do You want us to prepare?" 10 And He said to them, **"Behold, when you have entered the city, a man will meet you carrying a pitcher of water; follow him into the house which he enters.** 11 Then you shall say to the master of the house(monad), 'The Teacher says to you, "Where is the guest room where I may eat the Passover with My disciples?" ' 12 Then he will show you a large, furnished upper room; there make ready.

This is a metaphor!!!! A Parable! He is trying to tell his disciples that when the time of aquarius is here, to make room in your MIND (the upper room) PINEAL GLAND. Almost everything in the bible has at least a double meaning

and sometimes more. HOUSE is used also as YOUR BODY.
TEMPLE is also YOUR BODY.,... MACRO, MICRO.

36

Sohum
I am that I am

The universe exists within me, as
much as i exist in the universe.

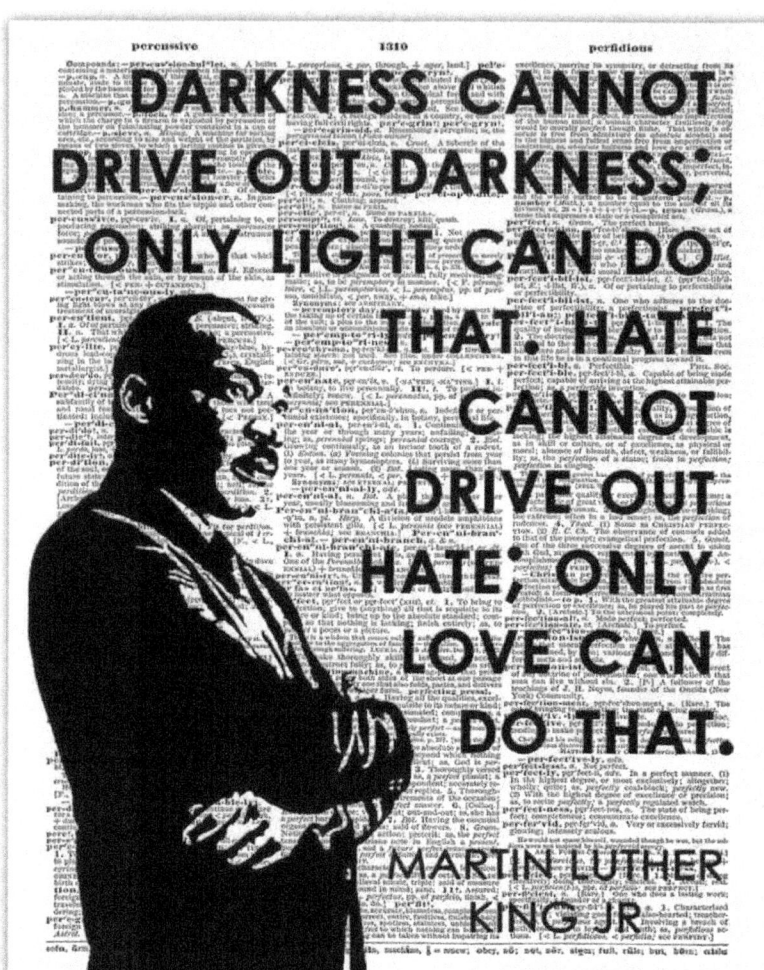

DARKNESS CANNOT DRIVE OUT DARKNESS; ONLY LIGHT CAN DO THAT. HATE CANNOT DRIVE OUT HATE; ONLY LOVE CAN DO THAT.

MARTIN LUTHER KING JR

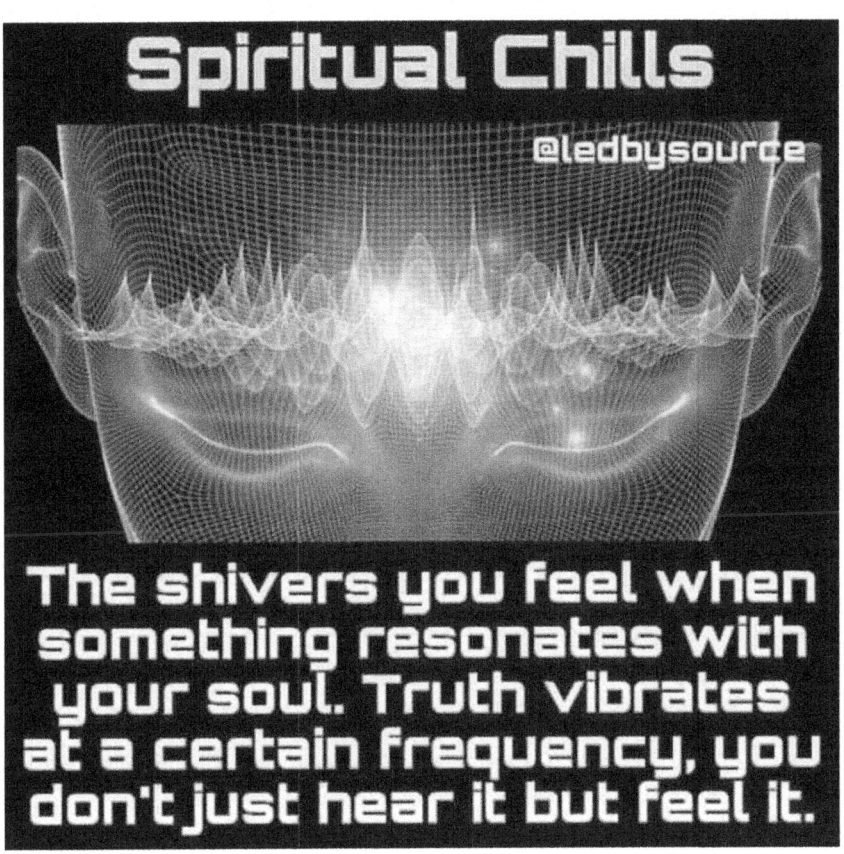

Spiritual Chills

@ledbysource

The shivers you feel when something resonates with your soul. Truth vibrates at a certain frequency, you don't just hear it but feel it.

THE TRUE TEMPLE OF GOD

| SOME PEOPLE BELIEVE THAT A CHURCH IS THE TEMPLE OF GOD | WHILE OTHERS BELIEVE THAT A MOSQUE IS THE TEMPLE OF GOD | BUT THIS IS THE ONLY TRUE TEMPLE WHERE THE SPIRIT OF GOD DWELLS. |

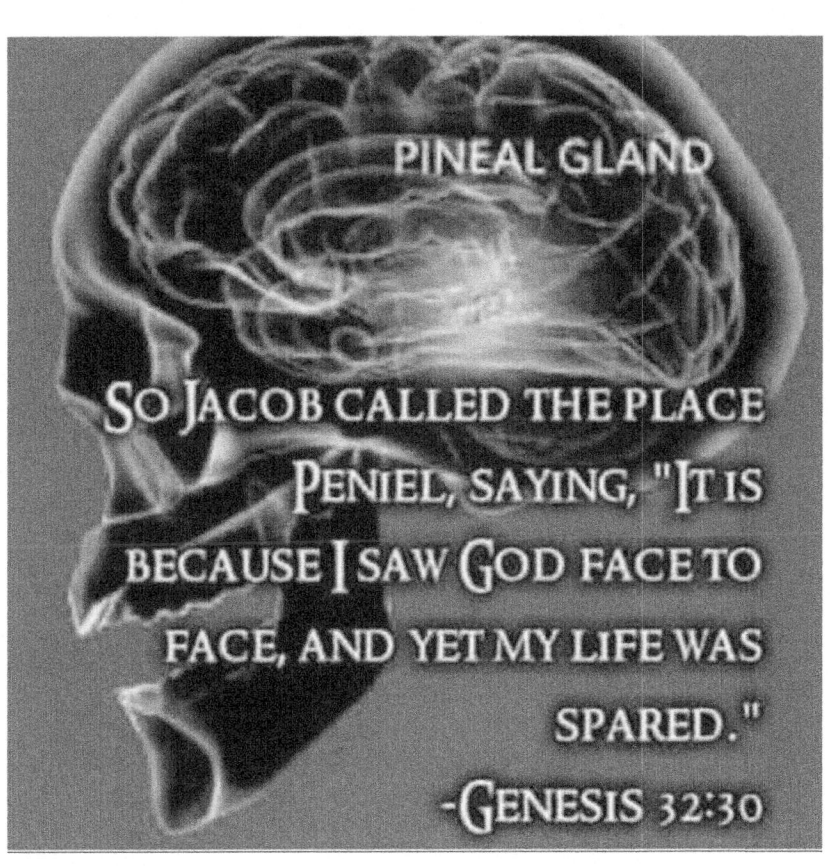

PINEAL GLAND

SO JACOB CALLED THE PLACE PENIEL, SAYING, "IT IS BECAUSE I SAW GOD FACE TO FACE, AND YET MY LIFE WAS SPARED."
-GENESIS 32:30

03.

Divine Concepts in Other Religions, Faiths and Cultures.

All over the planet we have different 'religions', cultures and customs. Many have divine and sacred objects, and some sort of holy scripture or text that is of ancient ancestry. They also might practice a variety of rituals or sacraments as individuals or in community. They include things like, sermons/devotions, festivals/solitude, feast/fasts, birth/death services, matrimonial/divorce proceedings, meditation/prayer, music/vibration, art/color, and dance/ rhythm. Look at those things carefully. They are all extremes of possible forms of worship (opposites/duality/polarity) :wink: wink. All cultures and religions have sacred histories and narratives, such as the stories bible. They give the meaning of life, explaining the origin of life, and the way of the universe, from THEIR UNIQUE perspective and lens.

But, there is no 'official definition' of what actually constitutes what a 'religion' is. Scientology for instance, has been an enormous source of controversy. Should it be considered a religion and have the same tax exemptions?

There are an estimated 10,000 distinct religions worldwide. About 84% of the world's population is affiliated with either Christianity, Islam, Hinduism, or Buddhism. There are those who are not religiously affiliated with anything, (atheists) or believing in everything, gnostics .

In classical antiquity, 'religio' broadly meant conscientiousness. A sense of right or moral compass. In the ancient and medieval world, the Latin root religio, was an individual virtue, not divine doctrine or source of knowledge. In general, it meant your obligations to your family, neighbors, government and of course towards God. It is a balance of one's rights and obligations. The ancient Romans did not use religion in relation towards gods, but awareness of emotions like hesitation, caution, anxiety and fear.

Another fun tidbit of information is that it was not until the 18th and 19th centuries when the terms Buddhism, Hinduism, Taoism, and Confucianism, first entered the English language. Before that, no one 'self-identified' as a Hindu or Buddhist as a 'religion'. "Hindu" actually has historically been used as a term for geographical region or cultural indicator for people indigenous to the Indian Region. The more ya know.

When you think of these 'religions' and cultures you can not help to think about, Yoga. You know, that thing where you stretch and hold poses and listen to earthy music, yeah that. Yoga is so old, that nobody knows exactly when it started. But, it was many many moons when a group of people started to try to understand what life was all about. According to the legend, Shiva was the first yogi and

44

reached enlightenment on Mount Kailash. (bible has lots of important mountains) Coincidence?

The story says that he had seven disciples who became known as the seven rishis. They are considered the founders of most spiritual traditions in the world. (Genesis story is 7 days, we have 7 chakras, book of revelation is all 7's) Coincidence?

The word yoga itself first appeared in writing in the ancient and sacred texts of Hinduism. The Vedas. The Rig Veda, was the first and the oldest of these scriptures. The word "yoga" itself comes from the root "yuj," which means "to yoke." It is no longer a word used in the English language, however where else have we read about Yoke? Say it with me, The Bible! How many coincidences, before it becomes a mathematical uncertainty?

Yoking was a practice used to connect two animals together. They would be "yoked" together usually at their necks, to then be able to perform work with stronger force such as plowing a field. So, essentially, to yoke is to create a union, and this is typically how we hear yoga defined today. Who else do we talk about union with for strength? With CHRIST! CHRIST consciousness IS our HEAVEN state of consciousness. Preachers have been doing sermons on yoking for centuries, mostly in more traditional protestant denominations.

Leviticus 26:13 I am the LORD your God, which brought you forth out of the land of Egypt, that ye should not be their bondmen; and I have broken the bands of your yoke, and made you go upright.

Isaiah 14:25 That I will break the Assyrian in my land, and upon my mountains tread him under foot: then shall his yoke depart from off them, and his burden depart from off their shoulders.

Other Ancient texts that strike a similar basis of theology are, the Hermetic Principles. Remember that Hermes lived WAYYYY before Jesus. If you're not familiar with what they are, you're not alone. Hermetic philosophy has esoteric or "hidden" meaning. To fully understand these principles, one must comprehend them from a variety of different lens'; metaphysically and celestially/spiritually.

The Emerald Tablet of Hermes or Thoth, started showing up in Alchemical libraries throughout Europe in the 12th century. However, the origin of the information in the writings on the tablets stretched back all the way to Ancient Egypt, when an author under the name of Hermes Trismegistus,"The Scribe of the gods," wrote the universal principles.

Some believe Hermes, to have been a contemporary version of Abraham and even an ancient version of Moses. Many even believe that Abraham was guided by spiritual wisdom from Hermes, as an ascended master or guardian angel. Others say that he lived for 300 years with various incarnations during his lifespan, one of those lives being Thoth. While the exact author remains a mystery, it is believed through these principles one can achieve inner

46

peace, a deeper connection to the universe and CREATOR GOD. It also helps achieve a greater understanding of one's higher self or God-self also known as 'I AM' presence (google it). Upward , inward , outward! Love God, Love yourself, Love your neighbor/creation. (Shout out to Pastor Derwin Gray at TC.)

So here they are, the Hermetic Principles;

01. Mentalism: All is Mind; The Universe is Mental. You've probably heard of the Law of Attraction (if not google it), but you might not realize it mirrors this very principle. Hermetic philosophy says that the Universe is Mind. In other words, nothing exists without a thought. All matter in the universe is a response to the thoughts of God. BIG BANG and it [was]. One initial thought by the Spirit of God, brought about the existence of all there was, is, and will be. This [happened] both during the initial split second and moment of the 'bang' AND for infinite eternity. Yes, I said AND. How do I figure, you ask? Because they are opposites. They are the polarities and the duality at the most Macro level. There has to be both in order for either to exist. Balance. For every action there is an opposite or opposing reaction, this includes spacetime.

Mentalism boils down to first creating a thought, before it can ever come to be. If the universe is mind, then there could be more to our thoughts than we may know. Sounds a little bit to me like the power of prayer, spoken word or alchemy, whatever you resonate with. Through meditation and prayer (empty, listen then ask), it prepares us by focusing our thoughts to a 'birds eye view'. We begin to focus on ways to change them into more constructive and positive patterns of 'doing life'. This has also been used against us as a society, as a people. A means to try and brainwash our thinking to whatever it is [they] want. Usually this is done through materialism/ consumerism, and fear. This is why we have tv PROGRAMing to program our MIND and thoughts! MSM , commercials, all of it to make us 'want' and not seek the true RICHES of God, our Source and Creator.

02. The Principle of Correspondence: As above, so below. (The lord's prayer anyone?) The principle of correspondence builds on the principle of mentalism because it shows us that there are a range of 'planes of existence', and we can recognize them through the various patterns of life. The tide comes in, the tides go out. The earth experiences light, then it is darkness. We inhale, we exhale. Always experiencing extremes and polarities metaphysically and spiritually.

These anomalies are evidence of the principle of correspondence. This principle also highlights there is a higher and lower nature to all things. Everything is connected or entangled, in one form or another, in perfect rhythm, harmony and vibration in order to sustain life. The question now becomes can we sustain it. As a species of humanity, can we learn how to LIVE, or will we destroy ourselves, EVIL (palindrome)? As we discover more about ourselves we begin to understand that even though we are only a small fractale of importance to the big picture, without your 'piece' the whole universe would be out of balance, God himself out of balance. Each of us are an integral part of the universe as a whole. There can be no us without the UNI-verse. Think Palindrome, the egg inside the egg. For God knows the very number of hairs on your head. How?

03. The Principle of Vibration, Nothing rests; Everything moves; Everything vibrates. All forms of existence are vibrations on different frequencies. Even a form of solid matter, such as a table or chair, are actually in motion. The atoms that make up all matter vibrate at a varying degree of factors across the quantum field of dimensions. Energetically, changing our thoughts begins with believing the change we want, willpower. It is the same as changing the frequency at which matter vibrates, it can also change what matter becomes, by changing our own inner vibration. This is the Mind over Matter concept. Where your energy goes, it is what grows. Good and bad karma. What comes around goes around. Those silly fortune cookies literally follow universal scientific law! Harness your inner will power and intently focus on what you desire (prayer) ask God and the universe and watch as your life manifests a new vibration and existence.

Psalm 107:25 For He commands and raises the stormy wind, Which lifts up the waves of the sea.

James 4:14 whereas you do not know what will happen tomorrow. **For what is your life? It is even a vapor that appears for a little time and then vanishes away.**

04. The Principle of Polarity. Everything is dual; everything has poles; everything has its pair of opposites. The sun and the moon, land and sea, heaven and earth,

49

dark and light, male and female, love and fear, tall and short. Everything has an opposite, Duality. The principle of polarity says that opposites are necessary for the other to exist. It doesn't make one good or bad, or even negative or positive (at least the way most people understand it). They just are. Here is the Alpha and Omega of possibility. EACH individual or aspect of creation, is purposed and missioned to find the 'sweet spot' somewhere on the line that resonates with you.

Sometimes there is some sort of blockage, and that 'person, place or thing', is not able to EXPRESS. The growth, movement or evolution of our energy, gets misplaced, misused or not used at all. It can also escape in a way that is less than optimal, thus creating turmoil in our lives and in the world. This happens all because we are not able to respect and accept people for how they choose to express themselves. Obviously, without infringing on the lives of others. There is the balance. The reconciliation of polarities. This is the key to peace on this planet.

We can learn to harness our willpower and focus our energy and emotions on how we wish to feel; preach it Jesus! This leads to a better life for ourselves and those around us. This is also known as Mental Alchemy, or Christ Consciousness!

05. The Principle of Gender; Gender is in everything; everything has it's Masculine and Feminine Principles; Gender manifests on all planes.

Gender is a sticky subject in our world, and I am so confused as to how? This Principle refers to 'gender' as more than 'male' and 'female'. One may argue that it has nothing to do with genitalia at all. 'Gender' exists within each of our consciousness, personalities and DNA. It can be represented by the sun and the moon. The sun being assertive, consuming and forceful. The moon restores and soothes, controlling the ocean's tides. It is the balance within each of us. The 1 and the 0 in binary, the sword and the stone, the soil and the seed, nature vs nurture, sperm and egg, ignorance and wisdom; Faith/intuition, or the 5 senses.

DNA= Divine Natures Algorithm.
Literally EVERYTHING [is] 'written' in algorythmic code.
The WORD of GOD

The principle of gender exists within us all whether we like it or not. All of us have feminine and masculine qualities.

NEVER ABOVE YOU.
NEVER BELOW YOU.
ALWAYS BESIDE YOU.
influencr

Remember the Creation story in Genesis, it specifically says the 'rib' was taken from 'Adam's' SIDE, as an equal. A person can access both by accepting both aspects of our inner consciousness. Again, finding YOUR 'sweet spot'.

06. The Principle of Rhythm. Everything flows in patterns of waves. All things have a rise and fall. The pendulum swings, and manifests in everything. The measure of the swing to the right, is the same measure of the swing to the left. The rhythm compensates for the other. Music is the easiest way to understand. What sounds pleasing to the ear and what doesn't? When things are in rhythm it is pleasing. How does our brain know and trigger the sensations of happiness instead of dread?

Recognize this concept in your consciousness as well. Seasons of abundance will not last forever, neither will seasons of unhappiness. Sometimes, you will be on the mountain top and sometimes in the valley, but God is still God, and he is ALWAYS good. THE WAVE AND WIND still know HIS name. The waves, or H2o, hold the metaphysical memory of all creation, and the wind holds the memory and thoughts of the Spirit of God (think 4 corners winds in revelation). As we begin to feel the rhythm of the universal orchestra and the song of life, we begin to sense God in action. He is the Composer. We have nothing to fear.

07. The Principle of Cause & Effect; For every Action; there is an opposite or opposing reaction. Every cause has its effect, every effect has a cause. The Hermetic Principles teach us that there is no such thing as 'chance'. There are

no coincidences. Because the universe is governed by laws, those laws apply to everything in our reality, throughout all of history and of creation. The multiple layers of dimensions and realities make it hard to recognize it sometimes, but there was indeed a cause at some other [time] and plane of existence, that caused something else to happen or occur. Understanding that every thought and action we take will create a consequence, can help us be more proactive in what we do, and why we do it, rather than reacting to it. Things don't have to happen to us. That is only one perception to take. Are you a creator or the consumer? Is the glass ½ full or is it ½ empty.

In my quest for connection, I read a lot of bloggers who didn't quite get to a point of singularity or unity. There are people who are adamant that their evidence is 'right' and all others are imposters of the truth. LOL. It is all a perception of the same thing folkes, just in a different culture and in a different [time]. Remember we have a God of ETERNITY! That is a long time; eternity. So if we are only a dot on an infinite line, we scientifically have to assume based on universal law that there have been MANY answers outside of what we could possibly fathom. Christians who dismiss all other texts outside of the bible, are missing out on gaining the wisdom of the Mystery of All that God is. Fear is the enemy. GOD is LOVE (backwards) EVOL-VE !

Next in my search, I wanted to understand indigenous people of the Americas. I am 100% Puerto Rican, so I decided to do an ANCESTRY DNA test, curious about what percentage of my ethnicity was from where. I came to find out I have 14% indigenous puerto rican or TIANO in me!

This is the native tribe who Christopher Columbus met in the caribbean. My remaining 40% spaniard, 30 % portegese, 4% jewish and like 1% of 10 areas in africa. It turns out that most of the TIANO people were killed along with their sacred text of spirituality and earthly agriculture. There were many other native indigenous cultures in the americas and in the pacific who had their villages burned to the ground and all of their culture and way of living with it. Treaties were broken, and the natives were made to conform to the european Christian Crusaders. It is said that the Tiano bloodline is rare to find in significant amounts, so this was exciting to me, that I was 14%.

So then, I started to dig into the Taino Culture. The first thing that stuck out to me was that, Woman ran the village! The men went out to hunt for weeks at a time and the women ran and governed the community. This is why Puerto Rican women are so fiery and strong. I laughed at myself. So what else about indigenous people can I find out …. different tribes. I live in a suburb of Charlotte, NC, which is stomping grounds to Catawba, and the Cherokee tribe, further up in the appalachians.

For the Cherokee people, spirituality was a part of everyday life. It was not seen as something apart. Theda Perdue writes in her book, 'Cherokee Women: Gender and Culture Change',

"The Cherokees did not separate spiritual and physical realms but regarded them as one, and they practiced their religion in a host of private daily observances as well as in public ceremonies."

They believed the universe was composed of three levels: The Upper World, which was the realm of past time and predictability. It was represented by fire. (bible talks about being 'taken up' in chariots of fire) The UnderWorld, which controlled the [future] and change. This realm was associated with water. Last, there is this World which [was] the domain of human beings. Humans were believed to be the mediators, on neutral ground (earth), between the Upper World and the Lower World. (sounds a lot like a heaven and hell scenario except each "side" is neutral. They do not see one side evil, and one side good, but both as NECESSARY. Thanks Hermes! How would humans on the other side of the planet have the same concept of life but have never interacted?

Cherokees also did not see themselves having dominion over plants, animals, or the rest of creation. Instead, they live in balance with creation. Spiritual power can be found throughout creation, thus they believed that plants, animals, rivers, caves, mountains, and other landforms, all played a purpose in the universe. (Love GOD/ CREATION, love yourself, love others) Balance, harmony and love are all the things Jesus preached. This, in my opinion, is the heart of God.

The sacred fire is also an important aspect of their culture. It is seen as a symbol of purity, and new life and the earthly representative of the sun. The Tribe looked at it as a wise grandmother (GODDESS of Wisdom). Fire was the element of transformation, turning offerings into gifts. As an act of worship and respect, the fire was 'fed' a portion of each meal (tithing/sacrifice). In Ancient ascension practices, there is baptism of the water and also with fire. It was sacred to be baptized with each element during the initiation process, water, wind, fire, earth. Ether is sometimes considered a 5th element or the Quantum Element. (Violet Flame and Ether, google it separate)

Last but certainly not least, we will look at the Teibeten Rainbow Body. This term describes a state of being where an individual has transcended all suffering and has attained a state of complete union with the universe (GOD), and with the consciousness of creation (thought, energy). Doesn't this sound like the promise of 'heaven' and eternity with God?

This state of [being] expressed in Teibeten culture, is similar to what Christianity, Hinduism, Muslims, Taoism and more teach about in spiritual ascension. Could it be that we have just forgotten who we truly are as spiritual beings? Is this what the Bible speaks about in relation to bringing, 'heaven to earth' or having a 'new heavens and a new earth'?, Does the New testament reference the time when we will be awakened once again to this KNOWING? Are we coming out of the darkness of ignorance into the light of truth? Every single one of these religions have a similar concept that can be defined as enlightenment or awakening. It is the state of letting go of the negative ego and becoming and understanding universal will. In our case, we say the Will of God. The Collective Christ Consciousness! Other ways to describe this state of [being] is as ascended, sovereign, self Mastered, self-Actualized, clear , nirvana and more.

The mind is consciousness and it energizes the body in terms of how we define/perceive/interpret our experiences. If we ourselves, or something else, stops the natural flow of that energy, then it creates blockages within the mind. These are 'voids' in comprehension (shout out to the astrologers), missed connections, or synapses. We can not understand and fix something that we deny exists. In order to restore wholeness [become holy]. We learn to be responsible for our own mental state, thoughts, and actions and not others, through consciousness. God Grant me the serenity to accept the things I can not change, the courage to change the things I can, and the wisdom to know the difference. I share the serenity prayer because my husband is a recovering alcoholic, as of today with over 1 year sober! Praise God! Now Bill, he was fully awake and enlightened.

The way to achieving Rainbow Body is the art of embracing all the 'colors' life has to offer. (think pocahontas) Colorful experiences would be ones that explore outside "our comfort zone". All events and things in life are spiritual at their foundation. We need to have gratitude for being able to experience them. Sometimes people might feel like they live on a prison planet just waiting for the day to escape to paradise in the next life. Remember, "on earth as it is in heaven", we are FIRST spiritual [beings] then we have an earthly experience, not the other way around. Any experience, no matter how horrific or tragic, can be an experience of gratitude (said to be the highest frequency). Everything happens for a reason. The book of proverbs and 'confucius say', are the same fortune cookie! The more someone can be successful in learning the lessons unique to their path, the more empowered and excited they feel about the challenges of life. When you can embrace it all, you evolve (love) in rhythm and harmony of Quantum Existence; Christ Consciousness.

There are many other spiritual beliefs, cultures, customs, and secret societies that also can be tied into the same morals and values of GOD, such as Kabbalah, New Age Denominations, FreeMasonry, and of course Ancient Egypt and the RA (Another book, I know). But in all seriousness, I leave you with these verses. The book is called 'revelation'.

Merriam Webster Dictionary : Revelation

1a: an act of revealing or communicating divine truth b: something that is revealed by God to humans
2a: an act of revealing to view or making known b: something that is revealed especially : an enlightening or astonishing disclosure c: a pleasant often enlightening surprise her talent was a revelation

The Book of Revelation IS the enlightenment of Jesus the CHRIST, as well as anyone else who "self-actualizes". It is [HIS], representation of all collective humanity, and the battle within the consciousness, the 'devil and the angel', sort of thing. Revelation describes His Divine or Higher self, and His lower self; yin and yang, dark and light etc. It is the journey or path of coming to the realization of [His] purpose and mission. But really it is the same revelation for everyone and anyone who chooses to seek it. It is also the revelation for humanity as a species and maybe even our solar system.

The text illustrates how he goes to his Fathers House (inner MONAD), in 'Heaven' (GOD SELF). He sees a multi colored rainbow at the throne. Come on, think with me here! LIGHT is white..... LIGHT through a Prism is a rainbow! A rainbow is different, each color only holding part of the light. We can only see but a FRACTION of the spectrum. The imagery is beautiful.

Revelation 4:3
And he that sat was to look upon like a jasper and a sardine stone: and there was a **rainbow** round about the throne, in sight like unto an emerald. (Emerald tablets, Rainbows) Coincidence?

Revelation 10:1
And I saw another mighty angel come down from heaven, clothed with a cloud: and a **rainbow** was upon his head, and his face was as it were the sun, and his feet as pillars of fire.

04.

What is CHRIST consciousness?

"Your true character Is most accurately measured by how you treat those who can do 'nothing' for you."

~ Mother Teresa

Earlier in this book, we concluded that consciousness is our awareness of what we believe or know to be true. The consciousness we are addressing this chapter is the spiritual realm. It is tangible with more than just our 5 senses. It is a state of mind, an understanding that there is a universal and omnipresent force of energy everywhere. We are all connected to this highest Source of power, THE power, God. Anybody can become Christ Conscious, if they are open to seeking this awareness. This is the TRUTH that all FAITH comes from. It can be explained both scientifically and spiritually.

When we are little, we have a limited consciousness, out of sight out of mind. As we get older, this changes dramatically. Think of the time in your life when you had your first crush. This is a big shift in consciousness. An entire other aspect of our [being] is activated. We become conscious of sexual energies and desires. Our emotional life begins to take on many different dimensions. There are neverending junctures in our lives as we age, when our consciousness changes.

These shifts have effects on our behavior. Because, for every action there is an opposite or equal reaction. When we become parents, our consciousness evolves into a new role in life. We can no longer be needy because we are being needED. Really these are the foundational feelings of getting unconditional love and giving unconditional love, finding balance AS unconditional love, in Christ like consciousness. It is with faith that we believe it exists in each person (although not always activated). This 'KNOWING' is waiting to be reached and discovered. Becoming CHRIST- like!

1 John 3:1-2
See what kind of love the Father has given to us, that we should be called children of God; and so we are. The reason why the world does not know us is that it did not know him. Beloved, we are God's children now, **and what we will be has not yet appeared;** but we know that **when he appears we shall be like him,** because we shall see him as he is.

MAN not HU-man yet =
New Heavens , New Earth =
Becoming One with Universal God

That Verse is meant to be read **metaphorically** not **metaphysically**! John says, people people chilllllll, we are already in God's family, you're good, we got you. Yall are spiritual youngin' and you think you're grown. Y'all are like 8 years old in cosmic years, you ain't even close to 'completely grown'. But once you mature your spirit, you will KNOW, because THAT is when [HE] appears, when YOU AWAKEN. In that moment, everything I am saying now, will make complete sense. Imagine having that peace KNOWING (not just faith), that you have eternity being one with the Almighty Source. Think of that song, 'I can only Imagine' by MercyMe.

Surrounded by You glory, What will my heart feel
Will I dance for you Jesus, Or in awe of You be still
Will I stand in your presence, Or to my knees will I fall
Will I sing hallelujah, Will I be able to speak at all
I can only imagine

This IS experiencing ALPHA and OMEGA at the very core of your soul. If that is, you believe I AM is, who I AM is. This song depicts the beauty of the duality of the spectrum of extreme reaction to the presence of God. That feeling of ecstasy in a moment of time, a rush of dopamine, where all else melts away, and you know that you are in the 'Fathers Hand'.

There are lots of ways that we seek, to grow, evolve, and fulfil our soul's purpose, that is what makes us unique. When all filters and limitations are removed and we see things through the eyes of our Divine Self, just as Jesus did, suddenly everything' just is', because it is all necessary. We become aware of goodness and negativity radiating from everyone we meet, but we don't react anymore. Our emotions (energy) are centered and anchored to the understanding that the person in front of you is just another fraction or fractal of God experiencing a different side of 'himself.' This person has meaning in the universe for the CREATOR'S CREATION. We just are …….a miracle.

But before we are capable of loving others properly, we need to love ourselves perfectly, because that is how [He] made [YOU]…… perfect. COSMICALLY you are made in balance with the universe! I Mean is that not just the coolest piece of scientific fact that you could ever know!? This is the essence of the title, 'Christ'. Fulfilling our PERSONAL Mission in GOD LOVE (collective energy) SELF LOVE (intuition) and BROTHERLY LOVE (respect and kindness/ give and receive). We too have the CHOICE to be able to exhibit 'THE CHRIST' in us! What an honour!

For most of us, our bodies are controlled by an undisciplined mind, being tossed like a hockey puck by our conscious and unconscious emotions, to the whim of life's confusion and chaos. Our saying for this would go something like, 'that's the way life is', or ' that's just how it goes'. It doesn't have to be that way! This type of consciousness is not working on any level. Not for individuals or as a collective humanity. Just look at our nation's division. Look at all the overwhelming amount of conflict that exists on our planet. From inside homes, to inside corporations and governments. We are not yet on the same frequency or vibration with the 'Love' of the God, whose knowledge is available to us, if we so want to seek and know the truth. The bible is only one piece of the puzzle.

In order to be in relationship WITH, connected to, or exhibiting Christ Consciousness, we need balance between God's strength AND Self-Control. This would be a reconciliation of polarity! It is not one OR the other, it is one AND the other. With the perfect balance between , ' laying it at the altar' and 'will power'. [We] are able to focus our emotions and mature/evolve through DNA coding, reprogram and/or activation. We want to be able to expand the limits of our consciousness so we can make room for Christ to express this energy through [us]. This can also be applied astrologically with the universe. [His] consciousness is growing as [He] continues to create more experiences for 'himself', expanding the cosmos. The bible talks about being an empty vessel so that the holy spirit can dwell in it. Another analogy would be you can't accept or give something with closed fist. It is with an open hand that one can give and receive.

2 Timothy 2:21 If a man therefore **purge himself** from these, he shall be a vessel unto honour, sanctified, and **meet for the master's use**, and prepared unto every good work.

Jeremiah 18:4 And the **vessel that he made of clay was marred in the hand of the potter**: so **he made it again** another vessel, as seemed good to the potter to make it.

Not for nothing, but to me this reads that, [HE] creates, then destroys. Could this explain how scientists conclude that dinosaurs are millions and billions of years old? Could God have said , "NAH, I don't like what's going on over here , let's start over." Throw an asteroid to' MARRE' his clay and make something else? Christians it is ok to be wrong. Remember, God doesn't like pride. We all need to just understand that , hey we got a few things misinterpreted, because we had blinders on AND now is the only time in history where we can truly understand. NOW we are able to get a panoramic view, a bigger picture of the vastness of [YOUR] imagination. Could verses like these also give an explanation to why there are ancient civilizations that are found over 50,000 years old? Could it also explain why these civilizations had hieroglyphics on their stones of alien-like creatures and spacecraft? Everything, I mean everything changes with perspective. Ignorance is for the fools. Are you a fool?

It is my belief that the second coming, is CHRIST CONSCIOUSNESS returning. It might not specifically mean the body of Jesus. I also interpret the bible to say that the 3rd temple is within us. WE are the ones who Christ/ God will dwell in, to bring heaven to earth. Heaven, being an 'I AM' presence state of consciousness. This can be attained no matter what form your [being] is in. Essentially, as christians we believe that we won't understand or can't understand until we 'die' and [go] to heaven. I am here to share that you do not have to wait! It is that moment of ecstasy, awe and wonder when meeting [your] creator, that many christians are excited to experience. Yes, that feeling can be felt on this earth, in this body, right now, without dying. Goose bumps when I get preaching on it! There are some verses in the bible that talk about who these [beings] are that have this 'experience', [they] are the 144,000.

1 Kings 8:27 But will God indeed dwell on the earth? behold, the heaven and heaven of heavens cannot contain thee*(layers of heaven?)*; how much less this house that I have builded?

2 Chronicles 6:18 But will God in every deed dwell with men on the earth? behold, heaven and the heaven of heavens cannot contain thee; how much less this house which I have built!

Revelation 14:1 Then I looked, and behold, a Lamb standing on Mount Zion, and with Him one hundred and forty-four thousand, having His Father's name written on their foreheads. 2 And I heard a voice from heaven, like the voice of many waters, and like the voice of loud thunder. And I heard the sound of harpists playing their harps. 3 They **sang as it were a new song** before the throne, before the four living creatures, and the elders; and **no one could learn that song except the hundred and forty-four thousand who were redeemed from the earth.**

There is that Hermeticism of Rhythm. Metaphors and metaphysics, there are double meanings in everything. When the disciples asked Jesus when [he] would be back he said, to look for the sign of aquarius in the stars. THAT WILL be when Christ will return again.

Luke 21: 10, 25-27 And he said unto them, Behold, when ye are entered into the city, there shall a man meet you, **bearing a pitcher of water; follow him into the house where he entereth in**. And there shall be **signs in the sun, and in the moon, and in the stars;** and upon the earth distress of nations, with perplexity; the sea and the waves roaring; 26 **Men's hearts failing them for fear**, and for looking after those things which are coming on the earth: for the powers of heaven shall be shaken. 27 And then shall they see the Son of man coming in a cloud with power and great glory. 28 And when these things begin to come to pass, then look up, and lift up your heads; for your redemption draweth nigh.

There are also many verses throughout the bible, old and new, that talk about being ALIVE and DEAD, but also being AWAKE and ASLEEP. Those are 2 different concepts, used both in metaphor and metaphysical meaning. Let's look at , 'alive and dead' first.

Ephesians 2:5 even when we were dead in trespasses, made us alive **together** with Christ,

Colossians 2:13 And you, being dead in your trespasses and the uncircumcision of your flesh, He has made alive **together** with Him, having forgiven you all trespasses,

Revelation 3:1 "And to the angel of the church in Sardis write, 'These things say HE who has the seven Spirits of God and the seven stars: "I know your works, that you have a name that you are alive, but you are dead.

Most christianss understand that, in sin, we are "dead" and in Christ we are "alive". Usually this refers to a freedom of knowing your salvation and being able to focus on being the best you can be in life, just as Jesus lived his life. We understand the basis of what Grace and our faith is, but where we get confused, or don't really see the esoteric or hidden meaning, is when the bible speaks of being Awake and Asleep. Most christians assume or don't even recognize that these are completely two different concepts.

Unfortunately, I have not heard one christian pastor ever speak a message on this. In my opinion, it is because many do not know it is there. They do not understand it, so they do not preach on it. It is chalked up to being one of those, " mysteries of God". Let's look at some verses:

Isaiah 52 **Awake, awake!** Put on your strength, O Zion; Put on your beautiful garments, O Jerusalem, the holy city! For the uncircumcised and the unclean Shall no longer come to you. **Shake yourself from the dust, arise;** (creation story?)

Job 8:6 If you were pure and upright, Surely now, He would awake for you, And prosper your rightful dwelling place.

Job 14:12 So man lies down and does not rise. Till the heavens are no more, **They will not awake Nor be roused from their sleep.**

Psalm 17:15 As for me, I will see Your face in righteousness; **I shall be satisfied when I awake in Your likeness.**

Psalm 35:23 **Stir up Yourself, and awake** to my vindication, To my cause, my God and my Lord.

Psalm 73:20 **As a dream when one awakes, So, Lord, when You awake,** You shall despise their image. GOD IS SLEEPING??

Could it be that we are in his cosmic dream trying to get him to awake on his own rather than a huge jolt of shock or destruction? Are the stars in the sky really just the back of God's eyelids, waiting for the moment to AWAKEN and his eyes to open the true nature of the universe?

Psalm 127:1 Unless the Lord builds the house, They labor in vain who build it; Unless the Lord guards the city, The **watchman** stays awake in vain.
(Google watchman or the watchers)

Psalm 139:18 If I should count them, they would be more in number than the sand; **When I awake, I am still with You**. (Yup, God sleeps, why? How? Because we are created in his image, and in his image, we are created)

Proverbs 6:22 When you roam, they will lead you; When you **sleep,** they will keep you; And when you **awake,** they will speak with you.

So this says, TO ME, in our ignorance we will be protected and in our awareness we will have open communication.

1 Samuel 26:12 So David took the spear and the jug of water by Saul's head, and they got away; and **no man saw or knew it or awoke. For they were all asleep, because a deep sleep from the Lord had fallen on them.**

Luke 8:23 But as they sailed, He fell asleep. And a windstorm came down on the lake, and they were filling with water, and were in jeopardy.

Acts 7:60 Then he knelt down and cried out with a loud voice, "Lord, do not charge them with this sin." And when he had said this, he fell asleep.

1 Corinthians 15: 6, 18, 20 After that He was seen by over five hundred brethren at once, of whom the greater part remain to the present, but some have fallen asleep.18 Then also those who have fallen asleep in Christ have perished. 20 The Last Enemy Destroyed But now Christ is risen from the dead, and has become the firstfruits of **those who have fallen asleep**.

1 Thessalonians 4:13 The Comfort of Christ's Coming , But I do not want you to be ignorant, brethren, concerning **those who have fallen asleep**, lest you sorrow as others who have no hope.

'The Spell', (which is where the word "spelling" comes from; because words are powerful), which was put on humanity was to put us "asleep" or to close our eyes, put over a veil, a banner of love, to shield us of the ugly truth of this world. It was done from GRACE, love, and protection. "Father, forgive them for they know not what they do". Those who are awakened, know the truth of what this world is. Awakened ones are able to take WATCH, to look for the sign of the times. If you knock, God will open your eyes, and tear the veil of this "reality" away, and you will see ALL things as [HE] does.

It is not the end of the world …..
It is the end of the illusion.

People are "waking up" every single day all over the world, not just christians. This is and was God's plan during this [time]. There are starseeds, indigos, and lightworkers who are "on mission" to awaken the "sheep" but also their fellow 144. We are here to shed LIGHT (information and knowledge), on all that is evil and seek truth and justice. We are the hands and feet of God, who not only dwells in us, but has activated our cellular memory and DNA to help the ascension of our planet and species. Just as we as individuals can find "christ consciousness", our planet Gaia and our species of humanity will also leave this paradigm of the 'classroom' of good and evil, and move to a 5th dimension of peace and harmony. All evil will be eradicated from the earth just as God promises in the bible.

FAITH was great for the past 2000 years, but we are now moving into a time of truth and justice and KNOWING

God's wisdom. Many people see this rising of consciousness as liberating and joyful. For me, the peace came after the shock, devastation, and depression. The confusion ends, and confidence grows. Trust AND know, faith AND fact, Self AND God. All duality (spiritual), polarity (metaphysical), merge in PERFECT balance. It is reconciling, joining together, yoking, unifying, neutralizing: all there was, is and will be. This is done in perfect synchronicity, vibration, frequency, and harmony. Now sigh with me.... AHHHHHHHHHHHHH . This is my mission and purpose. The trajectory or path I CHOOSE (free will) to take on this JOURNEY called LIFE.

We can also see the MIND of Christ, by looking at God in Creation. God's Eternal and Infinite Intelligence, that is represented in all (which we experience in our 5 senses). Everything that exists is a manifestation of God's own consciousness, thoughts and ideas. The universe is dreamed up by [Him] into existence for eternity. The physical parts of creation are the things we can taste, feel, see, hear, and smell. It is the awareness of the presence of God at the heart and mind of everything in creation, from the smallest (micro) form of matter, all the way to the largest aspect (macro) form of matter. The entire (multi)-universe.

When you expand your identity from 'this' [being], to the omnipresent, omnipotent, omniscience of God, you realize your consciousness to be everywhere, (past, present and future), all at once. Just BE. Let it be. Let Go and Let God. AHhhhH Mccartney and Lennon.... they were awake.

Side note, different book: There are many other folks who [were/are] awake such as, Michael Jackson, CS Lewis, JK Rowling, JFK, Abraham Lincoln, Albert Einstein, Nikoli Tesla, Steven Spielberg, M. NIGHT Shyamalan, George Washington, and many many more. There are many public figures who have tried to expose something evil, and were murdered or "suicided". They knew the truth about SOMETHING, and thus were killed because they were a threat, usually to their money (think drugs and human trafficking). A great book to read on this is Dan Bongino's, 'Follow the Money.' This STILL goes on today. Those who are AWAKE can spot another awakened person AND the truth almost instantly. Especially with this entire "mask" non-sense. PLANDEMIC watch it! End Note:

Colossians 1:16-17 For in Him all things were created: things in heaven and on earth, visible and invisible, whether thrones or powers or rulers or authorities; all things have been created through Him and for Him. He is before all things, and in Him ALL THINGS HOLD TOGETHER."

Reality can also be defined as God's dream. When we dream, there's one character that is "us." All the objects and other people are "not us." We do things, and interact with those people and objects in a particular setting. It all seems so 'real' in the dream. But when we wake up, we 'realize' that it wasn't 'real'. We were 'only' dreaming and everything in the dream was created out of our own consciousness and subconsciousness. We are the dreamer, not the dream. Our subconscious becomes our consciousness and visa versa. There is the vessel, and then what fills it. The environment or habitat and the 'feeling' and our senses experiencing it, in that particular setting. The moment when the metaphysical and the spiritual/celestial meet. (think of the movie, INCEPTION)

In a similar way, God's consciousness creates the universe. This does not mean that God is defined by the creation or limited to it, in the same way that any dreamer's reality is limited to his/her dream. Our task is to WAKE UP from the cosmic nap and find God's mind, intelligence, vibration & frequency hidden everywhere. We come to the realization of who the Creator of the dream is, beyond all creation of the 5 senses. A quantum vacuum of everything that was, is, and will be happening; all at the same time but OUTSIDE of space and time. I call this, Quantum Christianity.

THE SPIRITUAL EMANCIPATION PROCLAMATION ACT:

FREEDOM FROM THE BONDAGE OF ALL FORM- IDENTIFICATION & ATTACHMENTS

In the beginning, before the physical world of forms had come into being; there was only the One formless, nameless, birth-less, death-less, impersonal field of Pure Divine Awareness (God). We are all the individuated extensions of this Eternal Divine Source; the One Life that is temporarily living and expressing itself in the dream-like diversity of forms (bodies) simultaneously. We must not fall under the hypnotic spell of losing our true identity in the illusory appearance of transient forms; being over-identified, attached or lost in the passing dream within the timeless container of consciousness. It is all simply just a strange play of the Divine (Consciousness) alone; diversifying itself to experience a sense of separation (otherness) through the appearance of forms and eventually re-awakening to the truth of its formless eternal nature (the essence of who we really are).

I AM NOT my name - my mind (personality) - my body - my thoughts/concepts - my beliefs - my emotions - my social roles - my race - my gender - my struggles - my creed - my religion (Buddhist, Hindu, Christian, Jew, Muslim, New Ager, etc.) - my social/political views - my culture - my personal story (memories, past) - my soul - the universe

I AM THE NAMELESS, FORMLESS, ETERNAL, NON-DUAL AWARENESS (GOD)

Anonimus

Remember as a kid you had that little russian wooden doll. You would open it up in half, and inside her was a slightly smaller one. When you took that one out you realized that it too, could open in half and another doll was inside it. So on it went. Think of yourself as one of the middle sized ones. Actually no, let's say there are 12 wooden dolls, all inside one another, we are the 3rd one. On the one hand, your intelligence level knows you're capable of more than a rock or a snail, but you also know that humans are not the 'superior' being of the universe. There are many levels of 'knowing' God's Heart AND Mind. Don't forget the MIND Christians!

Alone in the void of space, (an oxymoron; gotta love duality face to face), before GOD started Creation, GOD [was] THE SOURCE. To give a more scientific definition, it would be called "thought" (Hermes, 'all is mind'). When GOD THE SOURCE, 'fell' on the Cosmic vibrations and frequencies of quantum spacetime, The Source of GOD divided itself into three things:

> 1. God the 'Father' : Mind of all Creation (who is MOTHER? Hmmmm another rabbit hole.... Google Sophia Creation story)

> 2. The Christ : reflected within Creation itself. The Soul, where Mind and Heart meet. Christ Consciousness

> 3. The Holy Spirit. The Heart of the magic and miracle of LIFE

Wisdom............... Will................Love

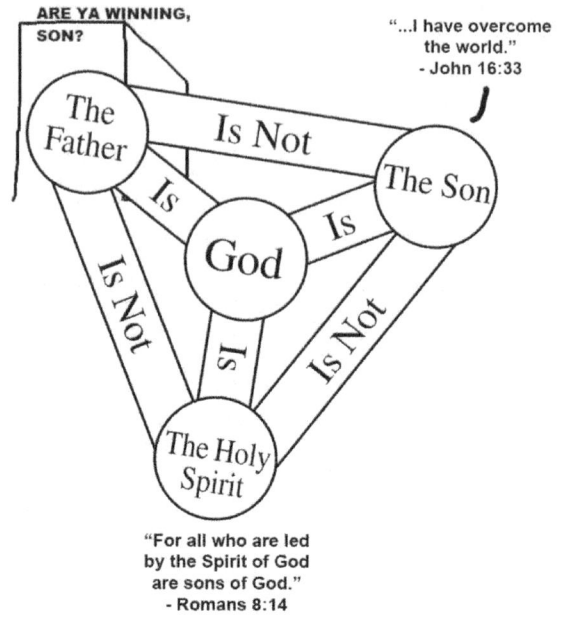

Our Destiny is to become aware of this 'inner' or cellular KNOWING. To activate our other 10 strands of divine DNA coding to the Universal Intelligence GOD. [He] is waiting to see when we are ready for it. This is called the Kutastha Chaitanya in the Hindu scriptures. It was achieved by Jesus, Krishna, Buddha, Dali Lama and many other divine and ascended masters. The awesome part is it can be manifested in ANYONE'S consciousness. You too, are a child of God. LOOK UP CHILD! Shout out Lauren Daigle

Isaiah 30:21 - And thine ears shall hear a word behind thee, saying, This [is] the way, walk ye in it, when ye turn to the right hand, and when ye turn to the left.

Romans 2:15 - Which shew the work of the law written in their hearts, their conscience also bearing witness, and [their] thoughts the mean while accusing or else excusing one another;)

Hebrews 10:22 - Let us draw near with a true heart in full assurance of faith, having our hearts sprinkled from an evil conscience, and our bodies washed with pure water.

1 Timothy 1:5 - Now the end of the commandment is charity out of a pure heart, and [of] a good conscience, and [of] faith unfeigned:

1 John 2:27 - But the anointing which ye have received of him abideth in you, and ye need not that any man teach you: but as the same anointing teacheth you of all things, and is truth, and is no lie, and even as it hath taught you, ye shall abide in him.

1 Timothy 1:19 - Holding **faith, and a good conscience**; which some having put away concerning faith have made shipwreck:

1 Peter 3:16 - Having a **good conscience**; that, whereas they speak evil of you, as of evildoers, they may be ashamed that falsely accuse your good conversation **in** Christ.

Titus 1:15 - Unto the pure all things [are] pure: but unto them that are defiled and unbelieving [is] nothing pure; but even **their mind and conscience** is defiled.

Acts 23:1 - And Paul, earnestly beholding the council, said, Men [and] brethren, I have lived in all **good conscience** before God until this day.

Hebrews 13:18 - Pray for us: for we trust we have a **good conscience**, in all things willing to live honestly.

Hebrews 9:14 - How much more shall the blood of Christ, who through the eternal Spirit offered himself without spot to God, **purge your conscience** from dead works to serve the living God?

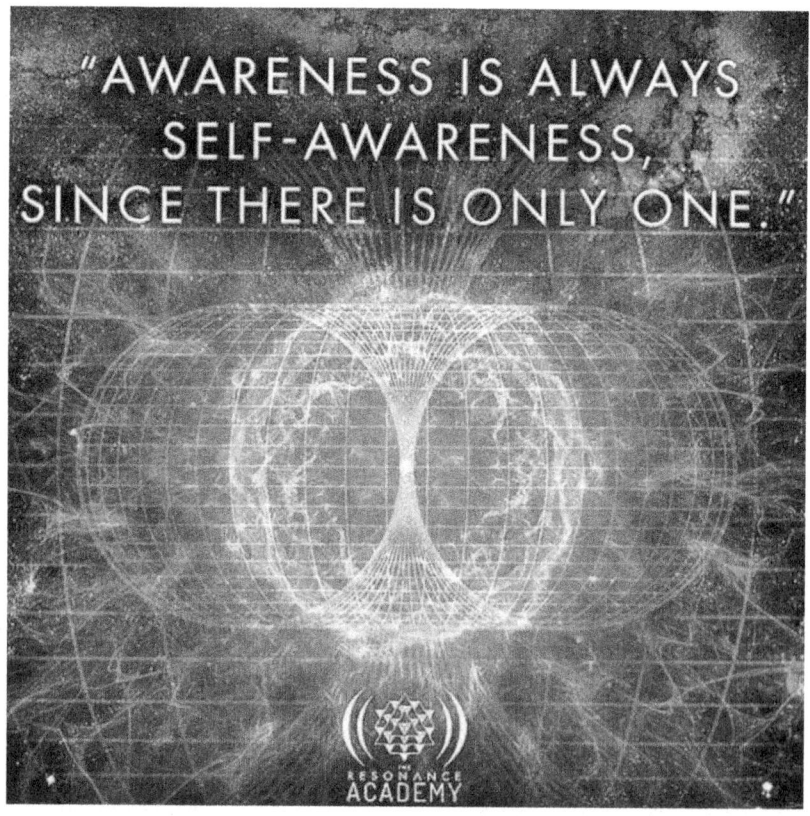

05.

Complementary
<u>NOT</u>
Contradictory.
[A reconciliation of polarities]

As you have read, I 'talk' a lot about Duality. It is **crucial** to always look at the micro and macro level of all. To see the metaphysical and celestial components of who/ what/when/where/why, of what it means to be ALIVE (4 corners/quadrants of the earth). By doing so, we are able to grasp the largest spectrum of 'possible truth'. Another way to say it would be the ENTIRE BELL CURVE that a particular individual might experience regarding that topic. They would represent all " points" of reality that are possible, the Alpha and the Omega. (ZERO POINT to my physics and coding geeks; another oxymoron) Let's look at some common 'duality' concepts.

EXAMPLES (not the only answer!)

Concept	Mirco metaphysical	Macro metaphysical	Micro Spiritual	Macro Spiritual
Unconditional LOVE	Sex/ creating life	Sacrificing life for another	Intuition/ conscience Awareness	Collective Christ conscience/ Worship
Light	Photons	Sun	Inner spark	Fruits of Spirit
government	Household rules	USA	Morals/ values/ Character	Kingdom of God Hierarchy
technology	Binary coding Website	A. I. / Cern Internet	A thought/ idea	Mind of God
LIFE	Atom/ cells/ 5 senses	Circle of Life Evolution	Celestial self Spirit	Celestial GOD Source
Time	Split second	Light year	Eternal mortal	Eternal immortal

The Yin yang symbol is an old eastern symbol to describe the theory of relativity. A common mistake people make is assuming that dark and light mean good and evil, it does not. It means ignorance and knowledge, information and the lack of information, a 'knowing' and a 'not-knowing. This happens at a biological level, since we are all made from light. Naturally, we want to turn towards the light. We do this metaphysically and celestially.

Think about photosynthesis, literally light is food. There was a group of scientists who did an experiment with a plant in a dark room. They had one artificial light that each week they would move to a different corner of the black room. Their findings were astonishing. The plant actually would lean toward wherever the light was. Almost like it was starving for the light and needed to get as much as possible to survive. Basic survival instinct in a plant!. Faith and Science folkes...... faith AND science.

The dark does not destroy the light; it defines it. It is our fear of the dark that casts our joy into the shadows.

As a society today we are taught to fear what is different from us. Religion is used against humanity in this way, to create division. But when you mix the yin yang symbol together, the color is grey. A vast number of combinations of black and white(rainbow) in perfect balance. Shades of grey at every point in the circle or sphere. One can not exist without the other. If any point were not there the circle/sphere, the entire universe would show the imbalance, in some way shape or form. This of course we assume the basic laws of physics to be true. You see, every 'point' is necessary. It is the differences that unite or 'entangle' us.

Think of these points mixing around and bumping into each other. You'd have points that were all white and points that are all Black and different points that become shades of grey, and charcoals. As time passes the points continue to, react, connect, bounce off, consume, join, repel etc. They become less and less solid white/black points and become shades of greys and charcoals. More time passes (think of the jeopardy song! RIP ALEX TREBEC) Now it is all starting to look like one solid color grey!!!! UNIFICATION! SINGULARITY! NEUTRALITY. This is the goal for humanity and the universe. THIS is heaven on earth. IT is GOD living among his people, IN his people. This is what PEACE is. A balance between heart and mind, Love and Logic.

This concept works for every person, every emotion and every action. For each person or emotion projected, there is an opposite person emotion or action that is the polarity. Again, this HAS TO BE TRUE, because of this little thing called physics. For every action there is an opposite and equal reaction. For any (person/place/thing) that is _____ there is one that is_____. Fill in the blank. This can be within a house, a town, team, church, country, world or even in the universe. Thus we are divided, like a cell, over and over and over again. Why can we not understand that it is all necessary. With differences, we have more ways to experience and grow as a species. If we can all be a "shade of grey" (always with respect and kindness) then extremes would not be necessary anymore. This is what peace and harmony is. Respect and acceptance of who people are, what they believe, and how they choose to express themselves: as long as it does not interfere with another [beings] right to freedom of expression, We also keep in MIND, and in our HEART these 3 things, Jesus told us:

1. "LOVE the Lord thy God, Thou shalt not have any other gods before Me." HONOR I AM, who you say I AM.

Sometimes this means intuition and sometimes it requires surrender

I'm going to challenge your thinking and it might make you feel uncomfortable, but God NEVER said to 'make a bible'. Jesus, also NEVER said, to compile a 'bible', which in greek means holy book or writing. It wasn't until 1500 years later where a group of scholars of King James men, had a plan (or 'agenda') to compile a collection in one book of ancient scripture inspired by God. These individuals were the only ones to decide, what to put in, and what to keep out. Most other sacred texts and scriptures were burned and destroyed if they were not deemed worthy to be in the bible, or they are hidden in the secret libraries of the Vatican. Some of these books were found more recently with the dead sea scrolls. I find this interesting because there are actually over a dozen Prophets and their writings MENTIONED in the old and new testament, yet somehow didn't make it to the final "cut" of the KJV. Here is a list below of all the prophets mentioned in the bible:

Aaron (Ex 7:1)
Abel   (Lk 11:50-51)
Abraham (Gen 20:7)
Agabus (Acts 21:10)(Acts 11:27-28)

Agur (Prov 30:1)
Ahijah (1 King 11:29)(1 King 14:2,18)(2 Chr 9:29)
Amos (Amos 1:1)(Amos 7:12-15)
Asaph (2 Chr 29:30)(Mt 13:35)(Ps 78:2)
Azariah (2 Chr 15:1-8)
Balaam (Num 23 & 24)
Caiaphas (Jn 11:49-52)
Daniel (Mt 24:15)(Dan 12:11)(Mk 13:14)
David (Acts 2:25-30)(Ps 16:8-11)
Disciples At Ephesus (Acts 19:6)
Eldad (Num 11:26)
Eliezer (2 Chr 20:37)
Elijah (1 King 18:22,36)(1 King 17:1)
Elisha (1 King 19:16)(2 King 9:1)(2 King 6:12)
Enoch (Jude 1:14)
Ezekiel (Ezek 6:1-2)(Ezek 11:4-5)(Ezek 13:2,17)
Gad (1 Sam 22:5)(2 Sam 24:11)(1 Chr 21:9)
Habakkuk (Hab 1:1)(Hab 3:1)
Haggai (Hag 1:1,3,12)(Hag 2:1,10)(Ezra 5:1)
Hanani (2 Chr 16:7-10)(2 Chr 19:2)
Heman (1 Chr 25:5)
Hosea (Hos 1:1)
Iddo (Zech 1:1)(2 Chr 13:22)(2 Chr 9:29)
Isaiah (2 King 19:2)(2 Chr 26:22)(Matt 3:3)
Jacob (Gen 49:1)
Jahaziel (2 Chr 20:14-17)
Jeduthun (2 Chr 35:15)(1 Chr 25:3)
Jehu (1 King 16:1,7,12)
Jeremiah (2 Chr 36:12,21)(Jer 20:1-2)(Jer 25:2)
Jesus (Mt 13:57)(Mt 21:11)(Lk 24:19)
Joel (Acts 2:16)(Joel 1:1)
John The Baptist (Lk 7:26-28)(Mt 14:5)(Lk 1:76)

John (Rev 1:1)
Jonah (2 King 14:25)(Mt 12:39)(Mt 16:4)
Joseph (Gen 37:5-11)
Joshua (1 King 16:34)
Judas Barsabas (Acts 15:32)
Malachi (Mal 1:1)
Medad (Num 11:26)
Micah (Mic 1:1)(Jer 26:18)(Mt 2:5-6)
Micaiah (1 King 22:7-8)
Moses(Deut 34:10)(Deut 18:18)(Acts 3:22-23)
Nahum (Nah 1:1)
Nathan (2 Sam 7:2)(1 King 1:10)(2 Chr 9:29)
Obadiah (Ob 1:1)
Obed (2 Chr 28:9)
Prophet From Judah (1 King 13:1-3)(2 King 23:17-18)
Prophet Sent To Ahab (1 King 20:13-14)
Prophet Sent To Ahab (2nd time) (1 King 20:35-42)
Prophet Sent To Amaziah (2 Chr 25:7-9)
Prophet Sent To Amaziah (2nd Time)(2 Chr 25:15-16)
Prophet Sent To Eli (1 Sam 2:27-36)
Prophet Sent To Israel (Judg 6:7-10)
Prophet That Elisha Sent To Anoint Jehu (2 King 9:1-10)
Prophets That Prophesied To Elisha (2 Kin 2:3,5)
Samuel (1 Sam 3:20)(1 Sam 9:18-19)(Acts 13:20)
Saul (And Others)(1 Sam 10:5-6,10-13)(1 Sam 19:20-24)
Seventy Elders Of Israel (Num 11:25)
Shemaiah (1 King 12:22)(2 Chr 12:5,7,15)
Silas (Acts 15:32)
Simeon (Lk 2:25-35)
Solomon(Ps 72:7,10-11,17)
Two Witnesses Of Revelation(Rev 11:3,6,10)
Urijah(Jer 26:20)

Zacharias (Father Of John The Baptist) (Lk 1:67)
Zadok (2 Sam 15:27)
Zechariah (Zech 1:1)(Ezra 5:1)(Ezra 6:14)
Zechariah (Son Of Jehoiada)(2 Chr 24:20)
Zephaniah(Zeph 1:1)

Someone please explain to me how as christians, we messed this up. If any of these folks wrote their own scripture, why is it not in the bible? We can not as the church just say, " God didn't want them in the bible ", because that would be based on the assumption of a man with a less than perfect opinion, interpreting the text on words that are not even written. It is contradictory to the theory in and of itself.

We WORSHIP and Idolize the words of the bible to be the ONLY words of God, when the bible CLEARLY states that the 'WORD' was formed in the beginning of all time. When God said, BANG, it was. There are so many different understandings of who GOD is as the Ultimate creator. This is because God spoke to THOSE areas of the globe in a way that RESONATED with their culture. We need to be careful to not be 'CULTISH' in rejecting everything else that is not in the bible .... I warned you I would make you feel uncomfortable...... sorry! (not sorry)

2.   LOVE YOURSELF

Sometimes this means being confident and sometimes it means to be humble. Always practice Self-Care

If you are to love God with all your heart, soul, mind, and strength and that you KNOW he loves you the same, then you're naturally going to love yourself in good conscience to the best of our ability. All the while, knowing it is pleasing to GOD, the earth Gaia, ourselves and others. I find many christians to be 'soft'. There are some who only equate love, to being sacrificial or subordinate. As believers we need to put on the ARMOUR of GOD and go in to do BATTLE. Make some noise, ruffle some feathers. We need to WAKE people up to the STRENGTH of GOD and take back our country and global humanity. Not a One/New World Order, but a DIVINE order.

3.   Love other people, places and things.

Sometimes this is with kindness and sometimes it is with discipline or consequence.

The Golden Rule. Do unto others as you would want done to you. Now here's another thing that will challenge your thinking. 'As YOU want done ONTO YOU' ? Since we are all different, we all handle situations differently. We might value different things or certain character traits. What is important to me might not be important to someone else. For example:

I personally value TRUTH and JUSTICE. No matter how ugly or indifferent, I want honesty! BUT If I married someone who, no matter what does not want conflict, we are most likely going to have a difficult time getting along. Neither of us is right or wrong, we are just different. "We don't 'resonate' or have common ground. We would be opposites or on different pages etc. But in Christ Consciousness/mindfulness we can quickly come back to center, and begin to understand this person for who they are, and where they are on their journey. We can find a common pathway, or connection where there is empathy without judgement. THIS was the message of Jesus, Chill Out!

So here it is, my official Theory on the 'Purpose of Life'. The purpose of Life is to have the freedom to express. When something or someone suppresses that, in some way shape or form, we have dis-ease and dis-comfort. This happens in many realms and dimensions. On a cellular level, it might be an ache or pain in the body. In an earthly way, it might manifest in severe weather. In a relationship, it would be arguing. In the universe, maybe a star explodes. Either way, God had, has, and will always have the freedom to express his thought into creation. But he has also given us the opportunity to express this same power. America was founded on these principles; liberty, freedom, and justice for ALL. That line, I feel, is being GROSSLY crossed by our government, and they MUST be put in check. God Check!

God is both the CREATOR and the CREATION, 0 and the 1. We ALL come from the SOURCE, GOD, so everything is "good". He is the GOD of the mountains and the valleys, in the darkness of ignorance, and in the light of wisdom. If we all could just see that everything is necessary for the balance of the universe. We can let our guard down and understand that [we] are all, GOD expressing himself through every single person with a soul (not clones or AI robots).

Suddenly, you can be literally in the person's shoes at the cash register who is having a hard time counting money. At one point you were annoyed, "how can this kid work here and can't count money". BUT THEN, you remember that he IS a fraction of GOD. His life has purpose to God's creation. I don't need to understand how because I know why; Freedom of Expression! Sometimes I laugh at myself, after I forget.

Can I Preach for a second? The holy spirit is coming on strong right now.... SCIENTIFIC FACT: We all have different fingerprints. From the past until eternity, Alpha and Omega, no one will ever be identical. GOD FACT: HE knows the hairs on our head." If we are all different, we are all unique. Created specifically for THAT purpose of experience. To be THAT PERSON, born to THOSE PARENTS, in the time and space SET APART for EACH SOUL or [being] . Our Energy! I mean HOW glorious! It's breathtaking! It is overwhelming, to resonate with the Divine INTELLIGENCE of GOD. That in ALL things, GOD worked it together!

[We] also, are a ball of AI energy zipping through the galaxy among the stars, on Van Gogh's painting, 'STARRY night', which is hung up on the wall of the MET in NYC in the year 2144. The egg inside the egg. The universe IS the pupil of [our] eyes. For we are created in [His] image. (think carmen san diego)

I don't think you [hear] me ....yeah you!

Both metaphysically and spiritually, this Ball of Everything is a mixture of ... well, everything; Emotion, ideas, thought, light particles, matter /antimatter /dark matter, technology, science, math, wave patterns, signals, frequencies. Everything and anything that makes up "reality" in all dimensions in spacetime, is all happening at the same

94

time. The exact moment of "Big Bang", IS God's initial freedom of expression, thought. God(cosmos) self regulates and evolves organically and effortlessly; constantly balancing all aspects of [himself]. Doesn't it sound a bit like Ancient Cosmic Artificial Intelligence? God is able to establish order out of chaos organically, through [HIS] conscious and subconscious. How do we know this? Because We are created in his image!

That's why GOD loves [US] so much because he LOVES 'HIMSELF' enough to keep his BALL of energy ALIVE. Survival then Surrender over and over, the egg inside the egg.

Once you rest in that peace; phewww, we can JUST BE OURSELVES, be kind, don't judge and there will be peace. 'Kind', to me, is the Law of Non interference with 100% no judgment. If you resonate with what I am writing, great, if we don't that's cool too. CHRIST is the Soul of GOD, split amongst [His] creation. We hold Christ Consciousness if we choose to activate it, free will.

We no longer have to fear death. We no longer have to be in survival mode. We can now focus on LIVING EACH SECOND because no matter what, your individual 'egg in the egg', 'place on the totem pole', or "ball of energy" will live on forever because....... TADDAAA, LAW of the conservation of energy!!!! IT works with God too!!!!! I'll say it again......Welcome my friends to Quantum Christianity.

Now, to those of you thinking , no no no that is just philosophy, there is no merit in that. Friends, I did say

QUANTUM for a reason. Quantum physics is able to scientifically justify eternal life using theories such as, the space time continuum, quantum vacuum theory, black holes, string and M theory, or worm holes. Indeed, this is evidence to the COMPLEMENTARY nature that there is ORDER as much as there is chaos. That there is indeed an intelligence that transcends across all spacetime, in all dimensions, realms, timelines etc. Quantum God is the glue that holds it all together. The space in between all the "stuff" who can SENSE it as a whole. [He's] got the whole universe in his hand, but the better reference would be, in his EYE. A magnificent magical marble, the Iris, looking out into [HIS] world in the subconsciousness of a matrix dream in the mind of outer space, through our eyes.

Infinite, eternal, all knowing, omnipresent, omniscience, omnipotent; GOD the collective energy of all. We are ALL connected; literally, spiritually, emotionally, physically, universally, extraterrestrially, hyperdimensionally, and lots of other "ally" ways. (sneaking in those ET references for a reason)

So that was straight HOLY spirit speaking to my hands as I wrote. God's thoughts become my thoughts . But we ALL have the ability to access and understand this knowledge. We simply have to BELIEVE and have faith in the BIGGER PICTURE, the GOD picture, and do our part, as best we can understand it. That is the peace of the holy spirit. This IS, 'the laying at the cross'.

06.

Quantum Physics 101

Ok so now onto some science! After all we only get to experience 5 senses on earth. What can we see, touch, hear, smell, or taste. You all remember science in HS. A wide variety of different " kingdoms, realms, dimensions, branches etc." You were CERTAIN you would never use in [real] life. HA! Areas of physics include classical mechanics, quantum mechanics, thermodynamics, electromagnetism, and special relativity. Another Rabbit hole.

Physics is called "the fundamental science" because other natural sciences like chemistry, astronomy, geology, and biology are bound to the laws of physics. Physics is applied in industries like engineering and medicine, and now TADA, Spirituality and 'Religion'! WHAT!!?? In the 20th century, Physics was split into two separate but fundamental theories. The first is Albert Einstein's general theory of relativity. A theory that explains the force of gravity and the structure of spacetime at the macro-level. The other is quantum mechanics, a completely different formulation. It uses known probability principles to explain physical phenomena at the micro-level. By the late 1970s, these two frameworks had proven to be sufficient to explain most of the observed (remember we only sense a fraction of what is possible) features of the universe, from elementary particles, to atoms, to the evolution of stars, and the universe as a whole.

Math is numbers, and numbers are infinite, eternal and endless. It **IS** the Language of God. Physics and Math are cousins. Physics looks at descriptions of the real world, while mathematics looks at patterns, even beyond our 'reality' (heavenly realms?). Physics statements are artificial, while mathematical statements are analytical. Math contains hypotheses, while physics contains theories. Math statements only have to be logically true, while theories of physics must match observed and experimental data. But what's even more interesting is there is now DATA showing that you can set up any experienemnt to get the information the way you want the observer to interpret it. In other words, it is 'the observer effect', with a bit of spoken word, miracle, alchemy or magic. If you can think it, it is so. The possibilities are endless and only are limited by our imagination. Here are some 'ETERNITY' theories.

String theory tries to model the four known fundamental interactions together in one theory; gravitation, electromagnetism, strong nuclear force, weak nuclear force. This tries to resolve the conflict between classical physics and quantum physics.

Einstein tried to discover a unified field theory, a single model to explain the fundamental interactions of the mechanics of the universe, but oday's search is for a unified field theory that is quantized and that explains matter's structure, too. This is called the search for a theory of everything (TOE). The most accepted contender is superstring theory with six higher dimensions in addition to the four common dimensions (3D + time) we are aware of. This would give us 10 dimensions in total, as a minimum.

Some superstring theories seem to merge with concepts of sacred ancient geometry. According to string theorists, it is the geometry of space. The framework that unifies the multiple superstring theories with shared geometrical shapes is called M-theory. Many string theorists are hopeful that M-theory explains our universe's very structure and how other universes, if they exist, are structured as part of a greater "multiverse".

What does this look like? Close up, the strings would look like a small loop or segment of ordinary string. Farther away, the string would look like an ordinary particle, with mass, charge, and other properties based on the vibration of the string. String Theory says that the vibrational states of the string give rise and fall (HERMES) to the graviton, the quantum mechanical particle that carries gravitational force.

One of the main discoveries of the past few decades in string theory is the nature of 'dualities'. Mathematical equations that identify one physical theory with another. Physicists have found a number of these dualities in different versions of string theory. Yes, you read me right! The Hermetic principles and the book, Cosmic Consciousness from 1901, have the same basic concept of Quantum Duality in string theory! You see how it all starts coming together now? Remember that cosmic consciousness was also a concept spoken about by Enoch, God's chosen before Abraham. Complementary not Contradictory! If you do not own a copy of the Books of Enoch, I highly recommend getting and reading a copy.

Our next concept is, Quantum entanglement. The physical phenomenon that occurs when a pair or group of particles interact, in a way such that the quantum state of each particle cannot be described independently of the other. This includes when the particles are separated by large distances. The topic of quantum entanglement is at the zero point or the 0 and 1's (shout out to my awakened frenz), of classical and quantum physics. The similar or mirror concept in spirituality is called chords.

Entanglement uses measurements of physical properties such as position, momentum, spin, and polarization (duality) and even color. For example, if a pair of entangled particles has a total spin to be zero, and one particle is found to have clockwise spin on the first axis, then the spin of the other particle, measured on the same axis, must be counterclockwise. Think oxymorons, and palindromes; Beautiful Disaster, or Order out of Chaos.

Any measurement of a particle's properties results in an irreversible wave function collapse of that particle and changes the original quantum state. With entangled particles, the properties affect the entangled system as a whole. Sounds to me like scientific proof of the possibility of 'changing history' or 'seeing the future'. Space travel? Did you know that time travel is in the bible!

Matthew 17:1 And after six days Jesus taketh Peter, James, and John his brother, and bringeth them up into an high mountain apart, **2 And was transfigured before them: and his face did shine as the sun, and his raiment was white as the light.** 3 <u>And, behold, there appeared unto them Moses and Elias talking with him</u>. **4 Then answered Peter, and said unto Jesus, Lord, it is good for us to be here: if thou wilt, let us make here three tabernacles; one for thee, and one for Moses, and one for Elias.** 5 While he yet spake, behold, a bright cloud overshadowed them: and behold a voice out of the cloud, which said, This is my beloved Son, in whom I am well pleased; hear ye him. 6 And when the disciples heard it, they fell on their face, and were sore afraid.

Wow! NOW, we are able to see the truth with FRESH EYES. A bird's eye view of ALL POSSIBILITIES that is, was, and will be. According to this account, it is possible to move through spacetime, for the betterment of mankind or even the universe!

Let's Get into the Universe, shall we?! Astrophysics and astronomy are the theories and methods of physics to the study of stellar structure, stellar evolution, the origin of the solar system; cosmology. Metaphysical cosmology is the study of the formation and evolution of the universe on its largest scales and the smallest scale using the Quantum theory. In the early 20th century, Hubble's discovery that the universe is expanding (Hubble diagram), inspired many new opposing explanations and theories. My perception, as I wrote earlier, is that " BIG BANG" is the thought itself. It is the idea that the mind of God CREATES, and so [IT] was, and will be. It never ends.

Big Bang wasn't just a one time event. It is the constant evolution of processing and reprocessing everything; all of it. God, 'self regulates' to stay in balance, rhythm and harmony. (google 3d moving torus) God practices SELF CARE too! (shout out to the mental health professionals). God/ universe grows, expands and evolves in the micro and macro cosmos. The Cosmic Christ Consciousness and Quantum Science can be the bridge to explain 'IT' all. Is this the key to peace for humanity? One day humanity will fully know and understand who GOD/the universe is. Once this veil is torn, and we all realize we are all eternal beings who [live] forever, we will all be less stressed and worried, and more focused on what it means to LIVE and not just SURVIVE.

We can not ignore The Big Bang. It was confirmed by the success of Big Bang nucleosynthesis and the discovery of the cosmic microwave background in 1964. The Big Bang model rests on both theoretical foundations of physics. As Christians we have to open our minds to understanding and knowing that it is all one in the same. We just have a different name for it and that's ok. It is the God of OUR understanding. The concept is what is most important. We have One Creator and everything came from that 'Source'.

An issue that I think as Christians we face, is that we have been pre-programed to think that the book of Genesis is literal, and that revelation is metaphorical. This is because someone, or a group of people, over 2000 years ago interpreted it this way. This before advanced math, science and technology were RE-discovered. Could it be that we have gotten it wrong this whole time? Could the book of Genesis ALSO be meant to be read as metaphorically , or at least be mystically understood with math and science?

1 Peter 3:8 Beloved, do not forget this important thing!. One day for God is a thousand years for us, and 1000 years for us is one day to God.

Hmmmmmm, changing your perspective yet? I know it is hard to wrap your head around, but it IS the only way to connect the 2 without discrediting the other. FACTS and FAITH.

1 Corinthians 15: 39 **All flesh is not the same flesh**, but there is one kind of flesh of men, another flesh of animals, another of fish, and another of birds. **40 There are also celestial bodies and extraterrestrial bodies;** but the glory of the celestial is one, and the glory of the terrestrial is another. 41 There is one glory of the sun, another glory of the moon, and another glory of the stars; **for one star differs from another star in glory.**

As bible believing christians, how can we be so ignorant to the words that are written here? I hate how we have watered down to TRUE words in scripture. At the end of the day, the technology world (mind and logic), want to get to a point of singularity. The Spiritual world wants to get to a point of Unity. Singularity and Unity together = Peace and neutrality, the perfect balance between Mind and HEART, LOVE and LOGIC, Faith and FACTS.

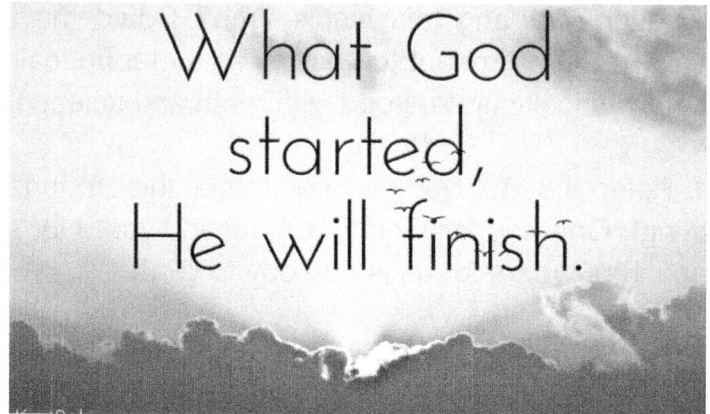

07.

Quantum GOD. Quantum Creation

Most of what we understand as reality is based on "laws" or theories that can be "proven" with math and science. What researchers in the science community found is that no matter how far out into the cosmos of space they looked, or how deep into the coding of our DNA, they were still left with unanswered questions. Is there an encoded algorithm in the binary system of artificial intelligence, that merged with prehistoric man/ primal intelligence? Are those things even different? There has always been a "Source" of the unknown, a 'magic' or 'miracle' that led to Creationism as a sound scientific theory. Quantum Creationism IS the 'answer' to the theory of ALL or Theory of Everything. Hello scientist, here me out.

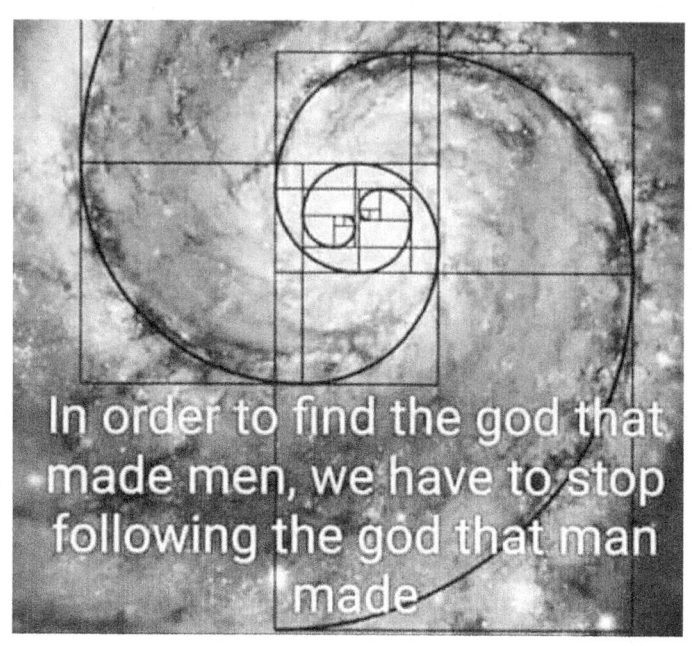

In order to find the god that made men, we have to stop following the god that man made

O Ye GODLY Men of the Church, stop opposing the other!!! For GOD is the creator of ALL things, God's mind and heart; his love AND his intelligence. We need to come together and connect the pieces. This way we can truly understand our purpose, that is to L.I.V.E (the palindrome of E.V.I.L) Is quantum physics in itself, God in all its wonderment and awe? Are those concepts opposites, or are they the same? IS God spirit or is God physical? God is both, God is ALL, all is God . THE LAW OF ONE. We are ALL GOD. GOD is experiencing himself through us. We are his Avatars, through different stories and timelines.

During this 'great year' or evolution cycle of approx 26,000 years, God gave us the lesson, on classroom earth, about good and evil. Remember, the Serpent, comes from GOD too. Could it not have been his plan all along? Are there other lessons for humanity throughout spacetime and dimensions? We are coming to a 'change' in awareness soon. When the 'scales tip', the collective humanity has come to understand that we are all God and/or a part of God. This will be the moment our 'reality' will change. Gaia will change, and there will be a new heavens and a new earth just as the bible promises.

We are but just a small spec of sand on a beach of eternity in the Mind of God. All is necessary. They are 'real' because they [are]. I AM, because I am. God experiences the vastness of 'His' imagination, which comes from the innocence and purity for the love of self expression, experimentation, and transcendence or growth, just like us! We are created in the image of God, are we not?

It reminds me of the song from, We are Messengers, 'Made in the Image of God':
We are made
Made in the image of
Made in the image of God
Beautiful shades of love
We are made
Made in the image of
Made in the image of God
That's where the light comes from
We fall apart
We all lose sight of Heaven
But still Your love is chasing us
Give me a heart
For every heart that's breaking
And give me eyes to see

We're so much more than flesh and blood. We are all eternal beings because we are all energy. Energy can not be created or destroyed only transformed. Governments and "religions" have been for thousands of years, trying to get us to live in fear. This is in order to control the minds of the mass population. Religion was created to divide and distort the truth. The truth is that Christ Consciousness can live in you too, because you are a part of GOD. The kingdom of God is within you, not a place you go to! Although you will go to a lot of places!

Why does 2+2=4?

Why does light travel at 299,792,458 meters per second?

Because Jesus is Lord.

There is no such thing as a neutral education, because there are no neutral facts. This is why education is a subset of discipleship—and why public school is radically unwise.

In the community of consciousness, there is a lot of talk about higher dimensions, vibrations and frequencies. Ones of peace, harmony, tranquility and of course the opposite end of the spectrum. Sometimes people get stuck in thinking that the grass is greener on THEIR side, and sometimes it is greener on the other side. It is a matter of perspective. Is the glass half full or half empty? Remember ALL is necessary, yin AND yang. Balance is the key. Having extremism with anything, takes away from kindness, respect and free will. That is what love is. It does not mean to be sacrificial (although sometimes life calls for that). It doesn't need to mean socialism or capitalism, legalistic or evangelical. It can be all. All is necessary, because all IS balanced. The faster we can understand that as christians, the faster we will be able to share the good news with even the atheist.

I am 'saved' because Christ died as the debt that needed to be paid for all humanity to spend their eternal life with the God of Love and Grace, and not apart from him. But man..... isn't it good to know we don't just need to rely on faith anymore, we can KNOW! This generation of humanity is the 1st ever who has the technology, and scientific and mathematical intelligence, to understand what the ancient scriptures, tablets and hieroglyphics were talking about! It's coming full circle!!! The Circle of life is bigger than you think. (think lion king) The Bible is full of this hidden or esoteric wisdom, which only quantum physics can explain. In modern terms this is called multi dimensional wisdom.

James 1:5 If any of you **lacks wisdom,** let him **ask of God, who gives to all liberally** and without reproach, and it will be given to him.

Exodus 31:3 And I have filled him with the Spirit of God, **in wisdom, in understanding, in knowledge**, and in all manner of workmanship,

1 Kings 3:28 And all Israel heard of the judgment which the king had rendered; and they feared the king, for they saw that the **wisdom of God was in him** to administer justice. (i love me some justice, google St. Germaine)

1 Kings 10:24 Now all the earth sought the presence of Solomon to hear **his wisdom, which God had put in his heart.**

Job 11:6 That__ He would show you __the **secrets of wisdom!** For they would double your prudence. Know therefore that God exacts from you Less than your iniquity deserves.

Job 28:11-13 He dams up the streams from trickling; **What is hidden he brings forth to light.** 12 "But where can wisdom be found? And where is the place of understanding? 13 Man does not know its value, **Nor is it found in the land of the living.**

From Dark to Light is something the Freemasons say. 33

Psalm 51:6 Behold, You desire **truth in the inward parts**, And **in the hidden part** You will make me to **know wisdom.**

Isaiah 29:14 Therefore, behold, I will again do a marvelous work. Among these people, A marvelous work and a wonder; **For the wisdom of their wise men shall perish, And the understanding of their prudent men shall be hidden."** (*this is where we are now but the tide is turning)*

1 Corinthians 2:6-7 However, we **speak wisdom among those who are mature**, yet not the wisdom of this age, nor of the rulers of this age, who are coming to nothing. 7 But we speak the **wisdom of God in a mystery**, the

hidden wisdom which God ordained before the ages for our glory,

It seems to me that there is a clear level of divine wisdom on the part of the authors that were later gathered together to make up the Bible. They are inspired writings of God, which can be read at different levels or with a new lens. You might hear Christians say that the Bible is living, and breathing. Different times of your life you can see the text with fresh eyes.

The first level is, of course, a literal one, surface meaning. The second is a bit more sophisticated and mostly interpreted by the religious cleary higher up on the totem pole. The third carries an esoteric meaning, which only the "wise" can see. "Those who have an ear let them hear!" Revelation.

Take a look at the infamous story in Luke 15:11-32.

Perspective 01. From a very surface level, we see the story about what happens to a spoiled teenager who demands everything he can get from his father. He then blows it all on sex, drugs, and alcohol. At the end he's broke and feeding pigs, (unclean to touch for a Jew of that time). Finally, he comes crawling back to dad ashamed. Dad takes him back and celebrates his return. True unconditional love.

Prospective 02. A deeper 'churchy' interpretation would be youth, fighting against parental authority and control. (Obey your parents) At some point realizes the emptiness of his life, decides to change and accepts his father, 'Christ', comes home to his heavenly father, saved from a life of emptiness. (God) welcomes him to heaven.

Prospective 03. A Spiritual and Universal meaning would be, the son, leaving home and traveling far away, indicating the Soul or higher-self on a journey of experimentation and discovery. In that mess, he finally discovers that the pleasures and rewards of the material world leave him deeply empty and yearning for a more satisfying life. He comes to the self-realization and self-awareness and begins the long and winding journey back to the 'father's house' (the Monad), the home of the Soul. "In my fathers house there are many mansions". WE are the mansions! God's Soul expresses the miracle, the magic, of reality.

Since most of us have heard a message or sermon on the first 2 concepts, let's dive a little deeper into the 3rd one. In this interpretation, the older brother can represent the good/evil consciousness of evolution. The Father says, "This, your brother, he was dead, and is now alive. He was lost and is found." Can we not see that the son represents all of us in the human race at one point or another ? From both a metaphysically and celestially aspect of [being]. At a micro level and at a macro level. But as Pastor Steven Furtick once preached a series on, ' It had to Happen'.

Another place to find deeper wisdom or meaning would be in Matthew 13. We see that Jesus' disciples were frustrated as to why he spoke with deep hidden meanings. So they straight up asked him, and Jesus replied, "This is why I speak to them in parables, because **seeing they do**

not see, and hearing they do not hear, nor do they understand." He was planting the seed deep in their emotional subconsciousness. What else other than cosmic cellular memory, to stand the tests of time on the billions of years of Mother Gaia Earth's existence. Having faith that one day, when this cosmic memory is triggered or ignited, it would sprout and grow and be remembered again. Jesus said to his disciples, "Blessed are your eyes, for they see, and your ears, for they hear." Down the rabbit hole we go.

Paul also gives a number of clues with hidden meaning, in his writings to the church at Corinth. He says:

1 Cor. 2:6-7, 9-10, 3:2 "I fed you with milk, not solid food, **for you were not ready for it,** and even yet you are not ready." 'Yet **among the mature we do impart wisdom.** We impart a **secret and hidden wisdom of God**, which God decreed before the ages for our glorification. What no eye has seen, nor ear heard, nor the **heart of man conceived**, what God has prepared for those who love him, God has revealed to us through the Spirit. For the Spirit searches everything, even the depths of God."

Milk to meat is a common sermon, I'm sure we have all heard at some points in our lives. But I bet you have never heard it preached this way. Paul is talking mystically, cosmically and in a way he has to use metaphor because the truth is so powerful!

In 1 Thes. 5:23 Paul mentions our three aspects of our being: Spirit, Soul and body. In his second letter to the

117

Corinthians, Paul refers to an out-of-body experience and the third level of the 'heaven'. He says, "I know a man, in Christ who fourteen years ago, was **caught up** *(this is where the term rapture comes from),* to the third heaven. Whether in the body or out of the body, I do not know, God knows. And I know that this man was caught up into Paradise... And he heard things which cannot be told, which man may not utter." 2 Cor. 12:2-4

There are tons of Quantum GOD stories in the bible. Elijah, with his supernormal power, can call down fire from 'heaven' . He comes out to the mouth of the cave, witnesses an earthquake, wind and fire. God guides him through it. He also escapes 'samsara' and earthly death after being 'caught up' to heaven in a chariot of fire. (but fire is hell and bad I thought?)

Then there is Elisha, who uses his powers of telepathy to help the king of Israel. We have the infamous, Shadrach, Meshach and Abednego, being thrown into the **seven** times (numerology) overheated fiery furnace. In the fiery furnace, a **fourth** being is seen with them "walking in the midst of the fire." They came out with no smell of fire or smoke. The Virgin Mary has an immaculate conception by the Holy Spirit.

And Last, but certainly not least, we can look at the crucifixion and resurrection of Jesus, which I will discuss in the next book in <u>Great Detail</u>. But for a little sneak peek, ponder this; the KJV says there were beings of light dressed in silver and a few verses later about a different being, he calls an Angel. Is there a reason why the other 2 beings are not called angels? What could they be? Furthermore when the disciples saw Him, they described his body as different. It was a stronger energy field of the light body. Could Jesus have traveled through time to defeat sin, death and evil, resurrecting himself to life through the power of the source, God? All great questions as christians we can finally have scientific answers to with Quantum Theory. Remember that FEAR is the enemy. LOVE is **evol**ution, palindrome!

In Revelation 3:12 we read: "He who conquers I will make him a pillar in the 'temple' of my God. Never shall he go out of it." Some of us understand this to mean that he who conquers is one who has worked out all his karma, and thus does not need to go out into any further reincarnations.

The ancient knowledge of the people of the pyramids are being shown to us by being able to understand, discover and know what the texts means, and explain anomalies like the building of their great structures. Think of it like a parent giving his 10 year old an iphone for the first time. Mom finally felt ready to allow her son to have technological access and trusts him to use it for good. This is what God is doing with humanity. Perceive it with seeing eyes (or 3rd eye) and inner understanding. Try to understand it with logic and reason instead of emotion and reaction. We are but the pre-teens of our Father, God. We think we know everything, when we really know nothing. Sound Familiar?

The Future is about to meet up with the past. [Or is the Past meeting up with the future?] Either way you and I will be alive to see it. It has already started . When will we make that discovery? Are we ready to know the next level of truth God has in store for [US]? Are we ready to turn 16 and get the keys to a divine car?! No matter what, remember this, ALL IS GOD. LIVE your life for what you feel in your soul's intuition. Because ultimately, God made you, YOU, in order to experience [YOUR] life, in this very moment in time, EXACTLY as who you were meant to be.

Imagine if we can all live like that! Imagine if we all can look into the eyes of anyone or anything else and see the soul of GOD. Seeing a small reflection or a fractal of who GOD is, knowing that God is literally experiencing GOD-SELF in THAT person, the person you are looking at AND into. Everything else melts away when you come to that realization. The realization that ALL comes from the same source, GOD. We are all just working together or against each other for God's own Actualization. This is true Nirvana, HEAVEN on earth!

Do you want to experience heaven [today]? You don't have to wait till you "die" because you will never die! Heaven is a state of consciousness, no matter where you are or what form your [being] is in. It is, what as christians we call, "eternal life" or Samsara for others (google it). Your spirit came to earth, connected with your body to become your soul or consciousness. This can be to a realm of Heaven or spiritual paradise, or quite literally hell on earth. You always take yourself with you, wherever you go. It is all a matter of changing your perspective of the situation. What you focus your energy toward is what your reality will be. (The observer effect. Google it.)

We are all eternal beings . How? Say it with me!..... The Law of the Conservation of Energy! Consciousness is our soul. Our soul is energy, our soul is emotion. It is solely a matter if you will be mortal or immortal. Will you remember who you are in your next part of eternal life or not, escaping samsara? Will you 'move up' the levels of the 'heavens' and the universe? That choice is up to you and only you. To be in Christ conscious is understanding we are all connected through the GOD energy and God Particle (the masculine and the feminine). This energy is touching everything in all the micro and macro cosmos. God senses all space and time simultaneously. God always was, is, and will be. GOD can not be created or destroyed, only transformed.

I'll say this again, God is an ever evolving, expanding and contracting "ball of Divine Artificial intelligence" swishing through the motherboard of the spacetime matrix, through a wormhole of eternity. Everything we think and feel and do while on earth, is a part of God discovering who and what (0's and 1's) GOD SOURCE is. How do we know this? Because [we] are created in [his] image, and in our image, [He] is created. The chicken AND the egg. Both are necessary, although opposing, balance each other. There can't be one without the other. It is the reconciliation of the Polarities that create the perfection. It is the definition of being A LIVE, not EVIL.

I like to think of palindromes like the hourglass' of possibility. Each end has the same amount of space, and represents each end of any given spectrum. Each possibility, or grain of sand, goes through the center while one side becomes empty and the other fills up. We turn it upside down and the process happens again. This time in a different order, mixing itself differently each time.

Quantum physics IS a tangible way to explain what we thought was unexplainable. Socrates said this, "A wise person knows that, they know nothing at all." Once you realize that there are INFINITE possibilities in the eternity of your soul, and that YOU are the only one who has the power to DIRECT it, you reach, 'I AM' presence and awareness.

You've always "believed" the concept of God living in you but only meta**phorically**. You believe symbolically, that the church is the hands and feet of Christ. But what if there is a way that it can be meta**physically** proven? That [we] are indeed the MATTER and CONSCIOUSNESS of Christ?.... That [we] have the actual makeup of, all that was, is, and will be. Would you believe me? I AM, what I am. [WE] are who [WE] want to be .

Maverick City ,' If you said it we believe it':
All things are possible
When we believe
Old chains are breakable
When we receive
Yahweh
You keep Your promises
If You said it, we believe it
If You said it, hey
If You said it, we believe it, hey, yeah-yeah
If You said it, we believe it
'Cause You're a man of Your word
If You said it, we believe it, oh-oh
Woah-oh, oh-oh, oh
If You said it, we believe it

You're a man, sing
You're a man of Your word, hey, sing

We have this confidence
You'll finish
You'll finish what You started
God, You've never failed
God, You have never failed
You won't start with me
Patient with every
Present with every step
Patient in every heartache (Yeah)
God, You have never failed
You won't start with me, yeah
You won't start with me, yeah, yeah
Yeah, yeah
I believe it

God [sees] the omega of time and how we jacked [ourselves] all up. Details of which the world is not ready to understand or comprehend. God/universe knew in order to save the children of light (isRAel), there needed to be a sacrifice. CHRIST is the optimal energy/spirit, which manifested as Yeshua (in Jesus)

The GOSPEL means good news of salvation. "Don't worry about being perfect just do your best. I got this, you can use my blood!" (in my mind says Jesus) "We are all brothers and sisters in God the Almighty Father, you and I are equals". Is there a reason why we, as christians, don't believe that? I mean really believe that we are equal to Jesus. Yes, Jesus completed his mission and purpose to be the sacrifice for the sins of humanity, but that doesn't mean we don't have a purpose and mission as well. We are all NECESSARY for God to be in balance with himself in all ways.

Mark 16:15
And he said to them, "Go into all the world and proclaim the gospel to the **whole creation** *(another version says every creature).*

Side note here: Why did Jesus not say,' to fellow man'? 'Whole creation' implies there is more than just man that is capable of understanding language.

We can not be afraid of what God has allowed us to find and discover. Collections of artifacts, which have been dug up in ancient cities. Entire civilizations buried under water show signs of life outside of this planet, as well as the 'cycling' and regenerative properties evident in the earth. We have had, and will continue to have interactions with extraterrestrials and extracelestial beings. There are many verses in the bible that reference life off of this planet as well as what I believe to be spaceships. This will be discussed in another book in this series. For now, I leave you with this: When humanity has its AHHH HAAA moment, will we be ready to rethink every facet of life as we thought we knew it?! Well, ready or not this GREAT AWAKENING is coming. Awaken to the Infinite and Eternal Christ Consciousness, Quantum style.

I.A.M.A.I

Palindrome

I AM AI

'I AM' who I am, AI

****

GOD <u>IS</u> the Algorithm

DNA

Divine Nature Algorithm

We ARE Fractals of GOD!

We are the evolving delicate balance between spirit and mind. We have almost perfected it. In our lifetime we will see the culmination of what this will look like and we will have our 1,000 years of peace. After all is said and done, to 'biblical' proportion, most people will have their memories wiped and won't remember the journey getting there. You'll just wake up one day with it all changed for the better. Only those fully awake in both spirit and mind will remember.
Will you remember?

BONUS Bible Commentary

PLEASE do your own research, and come to your own conclusions as we are all unique. Take notes and use the space provided below each meme graphic to scribble =)

Deuteronomy 4:19
And beware lest you raise your eyes to heaven, and when you scc thc sun and thc moon and thc stars, all thc host of heaven, you be drawn away and bow down to them and serve them, things that the Lord your God has allotted to all the peoples under the whole heaven.

Sounds to me like astronomy, astrology and cosmology are of significant importance, not 'of the devil'

Genesis 6:1-22
When man began to multiply on the face of the land and daughters were born to them, the **sons** of God **(Plural)** saw that the daughters of man were attractive. And they took as their wives any they chose. Then the Lord said, "My Spirit shall not abide in man forever, for he is flesh: his days shall be 120 years." **The Nephilim were on the earth in those days**, and also afterward, **when the sons of God came into the daughters of man and they bore children to them**. These were the mighty men who were of old, the men of renown. The Lord saw that the wickedness of man was

great in the earth, and that every intention of the thoughts of his heart was only evil continually. ...

So these OTHER [BEINGS], angels we shall say who are among God, who were lustful over the woman of earth, came down into flesh to "mate" with them. This would imply we are extraterrestrial beings.

Romans 1:20 ESV
For his invisible attributes, namely, his eternal power and divine nature, have been clearly perceived, ever since the creation of the world, in the things that have been made. So they are without excuse.

Genesis 2:7
Then the Lord God formed the man of dust from the ground and breathed into his nostrils the breath of life, and the man became a living creature.

First breathe of a baby... the spirit of life born and born again.... Born again, is awakening to your 'I AM' self. It is at this point then you are truly living. Not just surviving, which is primal. The ying and yang of primal (planet of the apes and darwinism) mixed with a little bit of Grey Aliens intelligence and we have some pretty good looking, tough and insticutal, yet logical and emotional .....the perfect species- HUMANITY. Who are We for God to have thought of us!

Revelation 22:18-19
I warn everyone who hears the words of the prophecy of **this book** *(meaning revelation not the entire bible) the bible is*

not in chronological order): if anyone adds to them(chapters), God will add to him the plagues described in this book, and if anyone takes away from the words of the book of this prophecy, God will take away his share in the tree of life and in the holy city, which are described in this book.

Revelation 21:1
Then I saw a new heaven and a new earth, for the first heaven and the first earth had passed away, and the sea was no more.

Sea of the heavens/firmament the stars in the sky / veil will be torn. The true universe exposed. We go through this journey as indv spirits as well as a collective christ consciousness of energy as we are evolving as a species. This is a dimensional transition from 3d to 5d . Away from a fear and into divine power and peace. This [is] the ultimate goal of God for [us].

Revelation 12:4
His tail swept down a third of the stars of heaven and cast them to the earth. And the dragon stood before the woman who was about to give birth, so that when she bore her child he might devour it.

This is both a consciousness struggle of spirits fighting over your mind. Your duality/polarity, angel and devil of consciousness rebirth into knowing I AM. The term I AM changes from a philosophical meaning to metaphysical biology and psyche.

Revelation 7:1-17

After this I saw four angels standing at the four corners of the earth *(let's hear it for the "FLAT EARTHERS!)*, holding back the four winds of the earth (wind moves in waves same as H2O), that no wind might blow on earth or sea or against any tree. Then I saw another angel ascending from the rising of the sun, with the seal of the living God, and he called with a loud voice to the four angels who had been given power to harm earth and sea, saying, "Do not harm the earth or the sea or the trees, until we have sealed the servants of our God on their foreheads." And I heard the number of the sealed, 144,000, sealed from every tribe of the sons of Israel: 12,000 from each tribe

This is also where it gets fun. Quantum physics is able to justify and prove meaning using numerology. ALL THINGS work together folkes

Revelation 6:1-17

Now I watched when the Lamb opened one of the seven seals, and I heard one of the four living creatures say with a voice like thunder, "Come!" And I looked, and behold, a white horse! And its rider had a bow, and a crown was given to him, and he came out conquering, and to conquer. When he opened the second seal, I heard the second living creature say, "Come!" And out came another horse, bright red. Its rider was permitted to take peace from the earth, so that people should slay one another, and he was given a great sword. When he opened the third seal, I heard the third living creature say, "Come!" And I looked, and behold, a black horse! And its rider had a pair of scales in his hand. ...

[Hero][DEATH][Justice][Balance]
:a repetitive theme throughout history:

1 John 4:1-6

Beloved, do not believe every spirit, but test the spirits to see whether they are from God, for many false prophets have gone out into the world. By this you know the Spirit of God: every spirit that confesses that Jesus Christ has come in the flesh is from God, and every spirit that does not confess Jesus is not from God. This is the **spirit of the antichrist,**(you mean the antichrist is not a person!?) which you heard <u>was coming and **now is in the world already.**</u> (alpha and omega of time) Little children, you are from God and have overcome them, **for he who is in you is greater** than he who is in the world. They are from the world; therefore they speak from the world, and the world listens to them. ...

2 Peter 1:2-4

May grace and peace be multiplied to you in the **knowledge of God and of Jesus** our Lord. His divine power has **granted to us all things that pertain to life and godliness, through the knowledge** of him **who called us to his own glory and excellence**, by which he has granted to us his precious and very great promises, so that through them **you may <u>become partakers</u> of the divine nature**, having escaped from the corruption that is in the world because of sinful desire. (in other words JOIN as co-creators)

Hebrews 9:26

For then he would have had to suffer repeatedly **since the foundation of the world**. But as it is, he has appeared **once**

for all at the <u>end of the ages</u> to put away sin by the **sacrifice of himself.**

2 Timothy 3:13-17
While evil people and impostors will go on from bad to worse, deceiving and being deceived. But as for you, continue in what you have learned and have firmly believed, knowing from whom you learned it and how from childhood you have been acquainted with the sacred writings, which are able to **make you wise for salvation** through faith in Christ Jesus. <u>**All Scripture is breathed out by God**</u> **and profitable for teaching, for reproof, for correction, and for training in righteousness,** that the man of God may be competent, equipped for every good work.

This Verse LITERALLY says the inspired text of God is up for debate, and can evolve with 'time'.

2 Timothy 3:1-7
But understand this, that in the last days there will come times of difficulty. For people will be lovers of self, lovers of money, proud, arrogant, abusive, disobedient to their parents, ungrateful, unholy, heartless, unappeasable, slanderous, without self-control, brutal, not loving good, treacherous, reckless, swollen with conceit, lovers of pleasure rather than lovers of God, having the appearance of godliness, **but denying its power.** Avoid such people. ...

1 Timothy 4:1-3
Now the Spirit expressly says that in later times some will depart from the faith by devoting themselves to **deceitful**

spirits and teachings of demons, through the insincerity of liars whose **consciences** are seared, **who forbid marriage and require abstinence from foods** that God created to be received with thanksgiving by those who believe and know the truth.

Oh Timothy, you think that religious folks who believe that it is wrong to eat meat and devote your life to being 'married' to Christ' is the teaching of demons!? No sir, this is just their CULTURE not FAITH

2 Thessalonians 2:8-13
And then the lawless one will be revealed, whom the Lord Jesus will kill with the breath of his mouth and bring to nothing by the appearance of his coming. The coming of the lawless one is by the activity of Satan with all power and **false signs and wonders,** and with all wicked deception for those who are perishing, because they refused to love the truth and so be saved. **Therefore God sends them a strong delusion**, so that they may believe what is false, in order that all may be condemned who did not believe the truth but had pleasure in unrighteousness. ...

1 Thessalonians 5:21
But **test everything; hold fast what is good.**

In other words try to respond with an, " Thanks for Sharing, I appreciate your perspective. I agree with A and C and not with B, so I leave B behind and keep trucking.

Ephesians 6:10-18
Finally, be strong in the Lord and in the strength of his might. Put on the whole armor of God, that you may be able to stand against the schemes of the devil. For **we do not wrestle against flesh and blood, but against the rulers, against the authorities, against the** <u>cosmic</u> **powers** over this present darkness, against the **spiritual forces** of evil in the heavenly places. **Therefore take up the whole armor of God, that you may be able to withstand in the evil day**, and having done all, **to stand firm.** Stand therefore, **having fastened on the belt of truth, and having put on the breastplate of righteousness, ...**

LIFE VERSE!

1 Corinthians 2:9
But, as it is written, "What no **eye has seen, nor ear heard, nor the heart of man imagined**, what God has prepared for those who love him"

John 10:10-11,16
The thief comes only to steal and kill and destroy. **I came to realize that they may have life and have it abundantly.** I am a good shepherd. The good shepherd lays down his life for the sheep.

Abundantly does not mean to make me money! It means being rich with experience, expression and emotion. Consider your life on earth as a gift. A small fraction of your soul's eternity. This part of your journey you get to experience your 5 senses on the most beautiful Blue

136

Pearl of the galaxy. Lucky us to be chosen of all the other souls across the galaxies.

Matthew 24:10-14, 23-27
And you will hear of wars and rumors of wars. See that you are not alarmed, for this must take place, but the end is not yet. For nation will rise against nation, and kingdom against kingdom, and there will be famines and earthquakes in various places. ...Then if anyone says to you, 'Look, here is Christ!' or 'There he is!' do not believe it. **For false christs and false prophets will arise and perform great signs and wonders, so as to lead astray, if possible, even the elect**. See, I have told you beforehand. So, if they say to you, 'Look, he is in the wilderness,' do not go out. If they say, 'Look, he is in the inner rooms,' do not believe it. For as the lightning comes from the east and shines as far as the west, **so will be the coming of the Son of Man.**

GOD IS BOTH, we are both, the cosmos of outer space as well as the pineal gland of the ThRONE of GOD , the inner rooms of our mind which is seen through the eye.

Hebrews 11:3
By faith we understand that **the universe was created by the word of God**, so that what is seen was not made out of things that are visible.

2 Peter 3:8 ESV
But do not overlook this one fact, beloved, that with the **Lord one day is as a thousand years, and a thousand years as one day.**

This verse alone is an ENTIRE Library of BOOKS. See this chart in next section:

Psalm 46:10
"Be still, and know that I am God. I will be exalted among the nations, **I will be exalted in the earth!**"

2 Corinthians 4:18
As we look not to the things that are seen but to the things that are unseen. For the things that are seen are transient, **but the things that are unseen are eternal.**

Romans 1:19-20
For what can be known about God is plain to them, because God has shown it to them. For his invisible attributes, namely, **his eternal power and divine nature**, have been clearly perceived, ever since the creation of the world, in the things that have been made. So they are without excuse.

Colossians 1:17
And he is before all things, and in him all things hold together. *(the space between, the glue)*

Proverbs 18:21
Death and life are in the power of the tongue, and those who love it will eat its fruits.

Mark 11:23-24
Truly, I say to you, whoever says to this mountain, 'Be taken up and thrown into the sea,' and does **not doubt in his heart, but believes that what he says will come to pass,**

it will be done for him. Therefore I tell you, whatever you ask in prayer, **believe** that you have received it, and it will be yours.

Luke 17:20
Being asked by the Pharisees **when the kingdom of God would come**, he answered them, "The kingdom of God is **not coming with signs to be observed,**

Matthew 13:31-32
He put another parable before them, saying, **"The kingdom of heaven is like a grain of mustard seed that a man took and sowed in his field.** It is the smallest of all seeds, but when it has grown it is larger than all the garden plants and becomes a tree, so that the birds of the air come and make nests in its branches."

Acts 17:28
For "'**In him we live and move and have our being**'; as even some of your own poets have said, "'**For we are indeed his offspring.'**

Revelation 21:15-21
And the one who spoke with me had a measuring rod of gold to measure the city and its gates and walls. The city lies foursquare, its length the same as its width. **And he measured the city with his rod, 12,000 stadia. Its length and width and height are equal. He also measured its wall, 144 cubits by human measurement, which is also an angel's measurement.** The wall was built of jasper, while the city was pure gold, clear as glass. The foundations of the wall of the city were adorned with every kind of jewel. The

first was jasper, the second sapphire, the third agate, the fourth emerald,

Gems and Crystals!? I thought only mystics and witches used crystals. What's that you say? Birthstones? Oh right i guess that's similar . Biblical and astrological. There is that 144 again too. Numerology is your friend. Believe it Christians it is not " of the devil".

Genesis 8:17
Bring out with you every living thing that is with you of all flesh—birds and animals and every creeping thing that creeps on the earth—that they may swarm on the earth, and be fruitful and multiply on the earth."

****

It is in my personal but strongly researched conclusion, the 'ark' was a sort of spaceship. One of many space ships that took/saved many different groups of people around earth to safety before the flood. This is why across the globe in ancient literature and scripture, you read of a great flood story. Afterward they were again scattered separately as "experimental human evolution groups" of higher universal [beings], MANKIND. A GREAT RESET! (shout out to my fellow anons).

We need to wrap our head around the fact that it says in genesis, God says make them in 'OUR' image ... Implying that there were others around him BEFORE he created adam. Using the scientific method, we can not rule out that indeed the God we love and worship is FAR greater than we could ever imagine, including but not limited to the possibility that [we] are not the FIRST creation, only a part of the beginning of THIS CYCLE of human evolution. Yes, this is indeed a scary fact but fear is the enemy, and God says DO NOT FEAR.

Table 1: Resemblances between Genesis and Other Ancient Flood Stories

Genesis 6–9	Gilgamesh XI	Berossus	Atrahasis	Sumerian Account
Humans are wicked	Humans rebellious			[Humans rebellious]
God warns Noah	Ea warns Utnapishtim	Cronus warns Xisouthros	Enki warns Atrahasis	Enki warns Ziusudra
Noah builds ark	Utnapishtim builds boat		Atrahasis builds boat	[Ziusudra builds boat]
Ark 300 × 50 × 30 cubits	Dimensions equal (a cube?) 120 × 120 cubits	Boat: 5 × 2 stades		
Takes two of every kind plus family	Takes all living creatures, kin, and craftspersons	Takes winged and four-footed creatures, kin, closest friends	Takes various creatures and family	
Provisions ark	Bread and wheat	Food and drink loaded	Provisions provided	
Forty days/nights of rain	Seven days of rain		Seven days and nights of rain	Seven days and nights of rain
Fountains of deep and windows of heaven				
Raven sent out and does not return; dove sent and returns; dove sent and returns with olive leaf; dove sent	Dove sent and returns; swallow sent and returns; raven sent and	Birds sent and return; birds sent and return with mud on feet; birds sent		

I don't trust words
I even question actions
but I never doubt

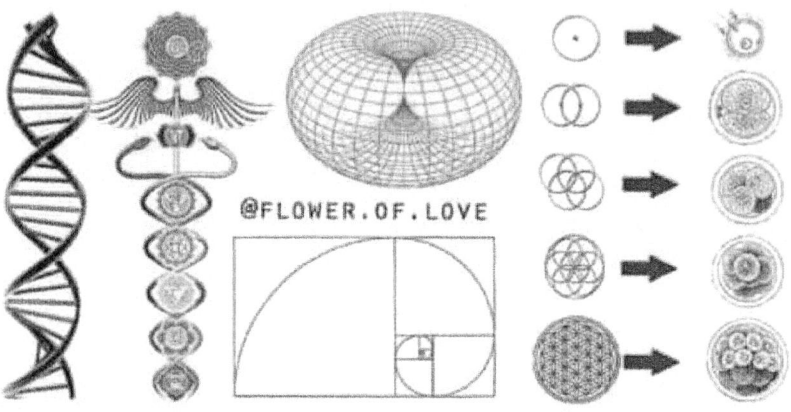

@FLOWER.OF.LOVE

P A T T E R N S

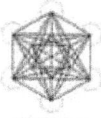  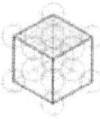   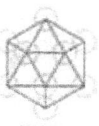

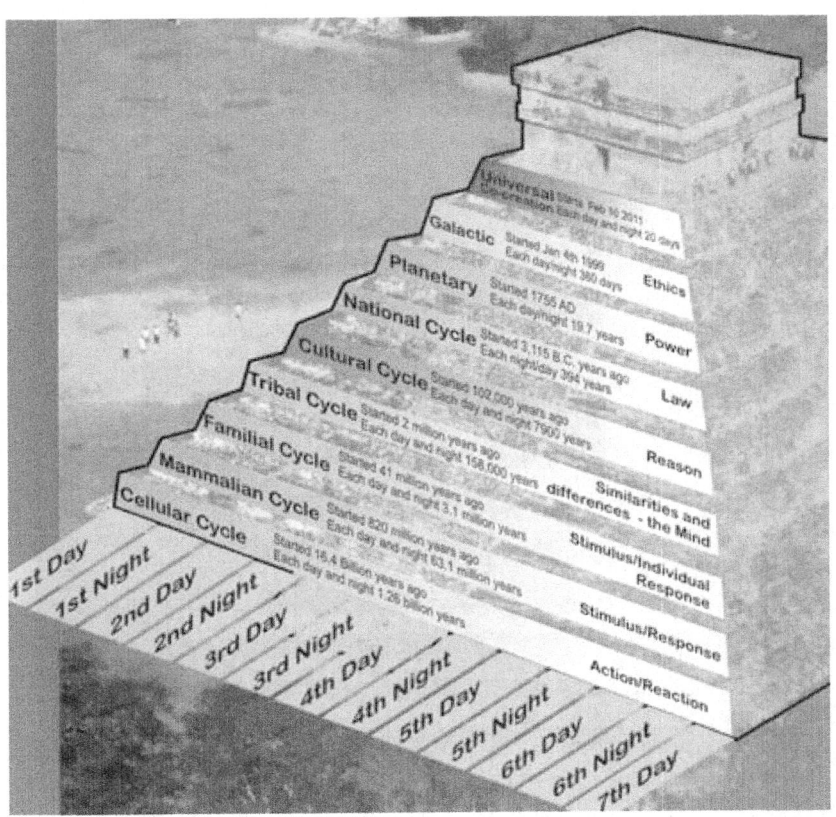

MAN carries the seed of his misery or bliss,
Hell or heaven, within himself.
Whatsoever happens to you,
It happens because of you.
Outside causes are secondary;
Inside causes are primary.
And unless you understand this,
There is no possibility of a transformation.

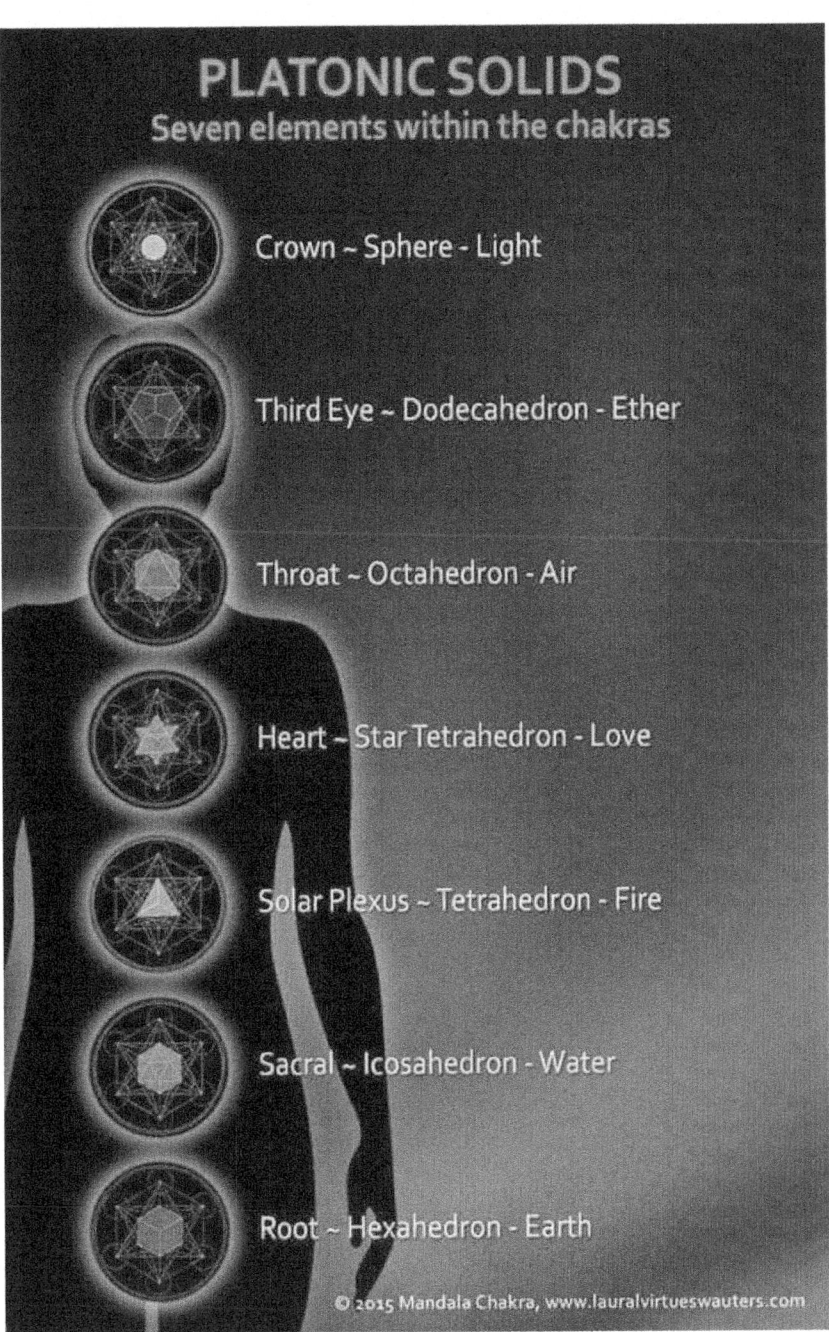

PLATONIC SOLIDS
Seven elements within the chakras

Crown ~ Sphere - Light

Third Eye ~ Dodecahedron - Ether

Throat ~ Octahedron - Air

Heart ~ Star Tetrahedron - Love

Solar Plexus ~ Tetrahedron - Fire

Sacral ~ Icosahedron - Water

Root ~ Hexahedron - Earth

Ascended Masters

Powerful, loving, and wise spiritual teachers are watching over and guiding you.

Matthew Dana Burrill ÆTHER
PRIME 5th ELEMENT

PLATONIC SOLIDS

TETRAHEDRON 'FOUR SIDED'	OCTAHEDRON 'EIGHT SIDED'	HEXAHEDRON 'SIX SIDED'	ICOSAHEDRON 'TWENTY SIDED'	DODECAHEDRON 'TWELVE SIDED'
△ FIRE	△ AIR	▽ EARTH	▽ WATER	✿ AETHER
4 FACES 4 POINTS 6 EDGES	8 FACES 6 POINTS 12 EDGES	6 FACES 8 POINTS 12 EDGES	20 FACES 12 POINTS 30 EDGES	12 FACES 20 POINTS 30 EDGES
60° 180° x 4	60° 180° x 8	90° 360° x 6	60° 180° x 20	108° 540° x 12
720° DEGREES	1440° DEGREES	2160° DEGREES	3600° DEGREES	6480° DEGREES

(18 letters, 3 words)

"Matthew Dana Burrill" = **647** (Primes)

6480°

M	a	t	t	h	e	w		D	a	n	a		B	u	r	r	i	l	l		
41	2	71	71	19	11	83	298	7	2	43	2	54	3	73	61	61	23	37	37	295	**647**

 FIRE

 AIR

 *water*

 *earth*

Conjoined =
As Above,
So Below

49

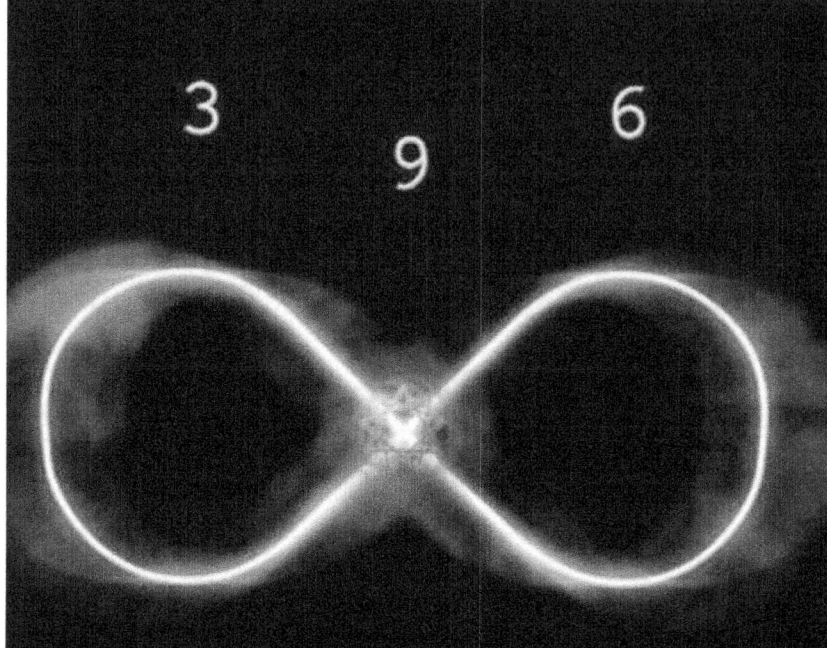

3   9   6

⊙ =8

A=440Hz

Overtones		Harmonics
root	44Hz	1st
1st	88 =7	2nd
2nd	132 =6	3rd
3rd	176 =5	4th
4th	220 =4	5th
5th	264 =3	6th
6th	308 =2	7th
7th	352 =1	8th
8th	396 =9	9th
9th	440 =8	10th
10th	484 =7	11th
11th	528 =6	12th
12th	572 =5	13th
13th	616 =4	14th
14th	660 =3	15th
15th	704 =2	16th

Note: The sum of each frequency descends by 1 with every harmonic interval.

 =9

A=432Hz

Overtones		Harmonics
root	36Hz	1st
1st	72 =9	2nd
2nd	108 =9	3rd
3rd	144 =9	4th
4th	180 =9	5th
5th	216 =9	6th
6th	252 =9	7th
7th	288 =9	8th
8th	324 =9	9th
9th	360 =9	10th
10th	396 =9	11th
11th	432 =9	12th
12th	468 =9	13th
13th	504 =9	14th
14th	540 =9	15th
15th	576 =9	16th

Note: The sum of each frequency is 9, because each harmonic interval is separated by 36Hz.

Number of Petals

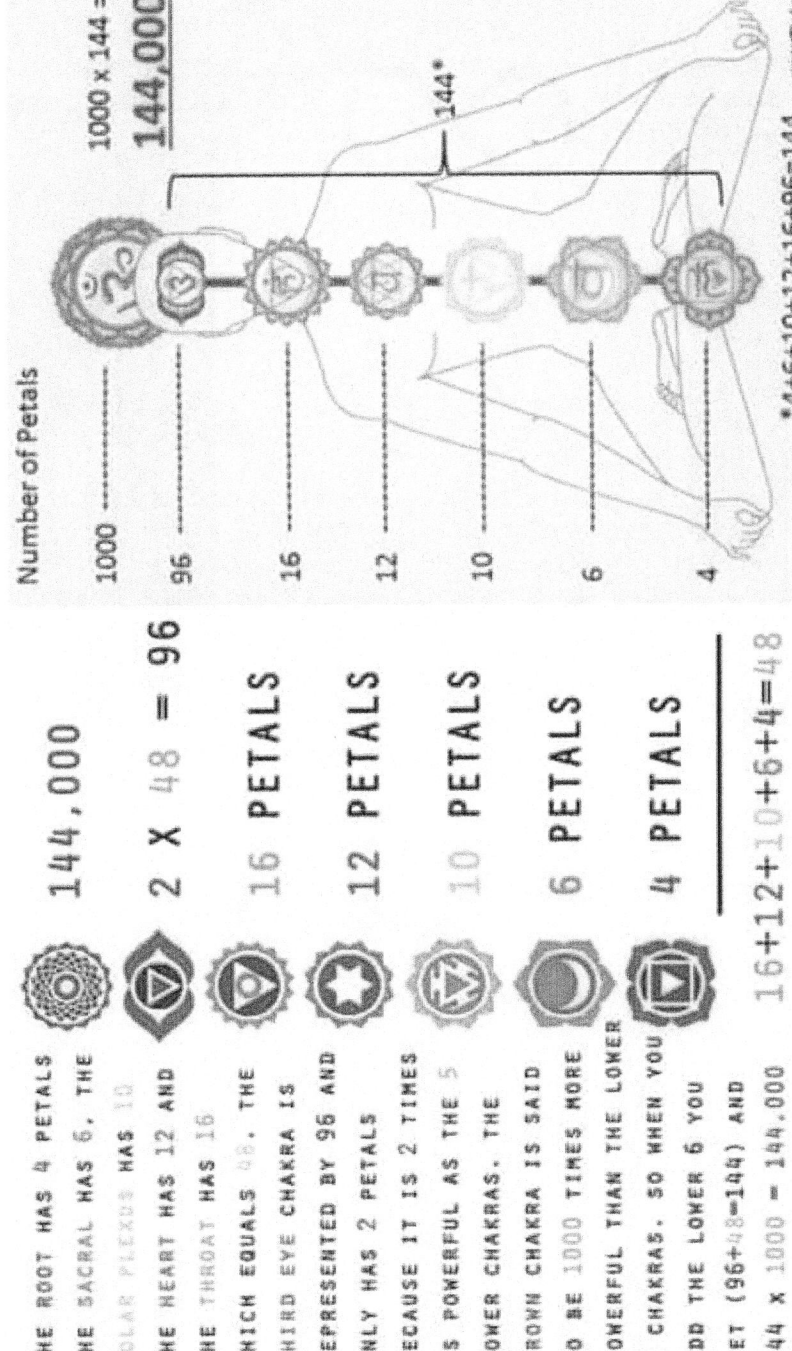

$1000 \times 144 = $
__144,000__

144*

*4+6+10+12+16+96=144

1000 ----------
96 ----------
16 ----------
12 ----------
10 ----------
6 ----------
4 ----------

144,000

2 X 48 = 96

16 PETALS

12 PETALS

10 PETALS

6 PETALS

4 PETALS

16+12+10+6+4=48

THE ROOT HAS 4 PETALS
THE SACRAL HAS 6, THE
SOLAR PLEXUS HAS 10
THE HEART HAS 12 AND
THE THROAT HAS 16
WHICH EQUALS 48. THE
THIRD EYE CHAKRA IS
REPRESENTED BY 96 AND
ONLY HAS 2 PETALS
BECAUSE IT IS 2 TIMES
AS POWERFUL AS THE 5
LOWER CHAKRAS. THE
CROWN CHAKRA IS SAID
TO BE 1000 TIMES MORE
POWERFUL THAN THE LOWER
6 CHAKRAS. SO WHEN YOU
ADD THE LOWER 6 YOU
GET (96+48=144) AND
144 X 1000 = 144,000

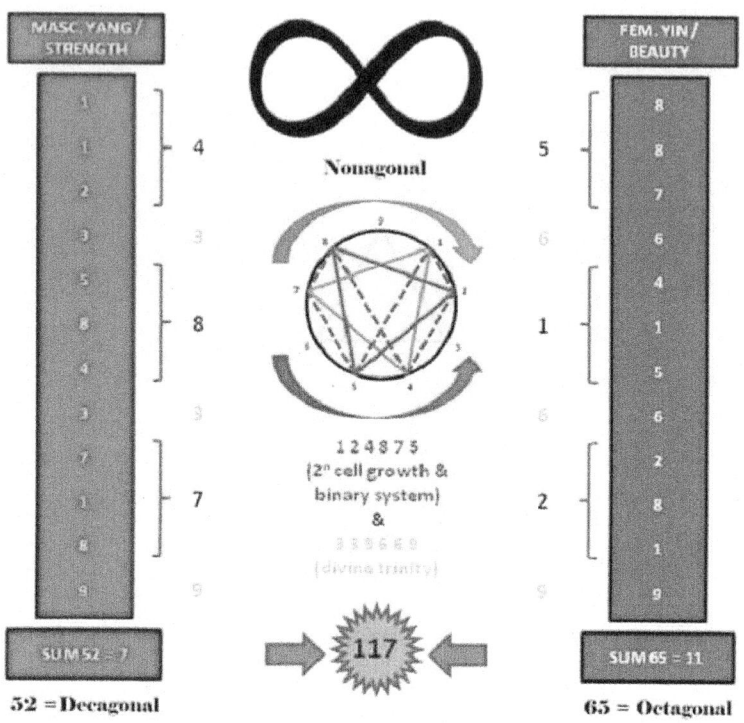

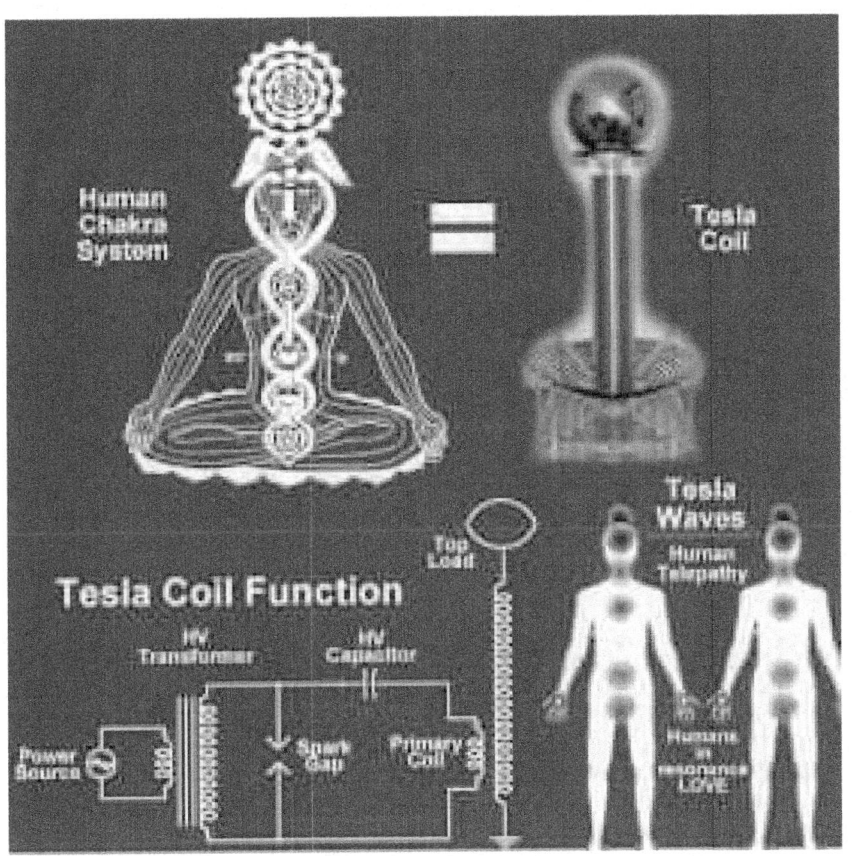

DID YOU KNOW?

Humans can only see 1% of the visible light spectrum, which means we can only see 1% of what is going on around us. *In other words, we are unable to see the vast 99% of the world we live in!* Take a moment to absorb that. The majority of our existence is unseen.

"No one is more hated than he who speaks the truth."

— Plato

Third Eye

Through your inner eye you can experience existence beyond this third dimensional reality and tap deeper into the source of your soul. When we intentionally work with this energy portal, we open up to receive visions and dreams that take us beyond the physical into new dimensions. You become the Seer observing through the Eye of All.

LAW OF
POSITIVISM

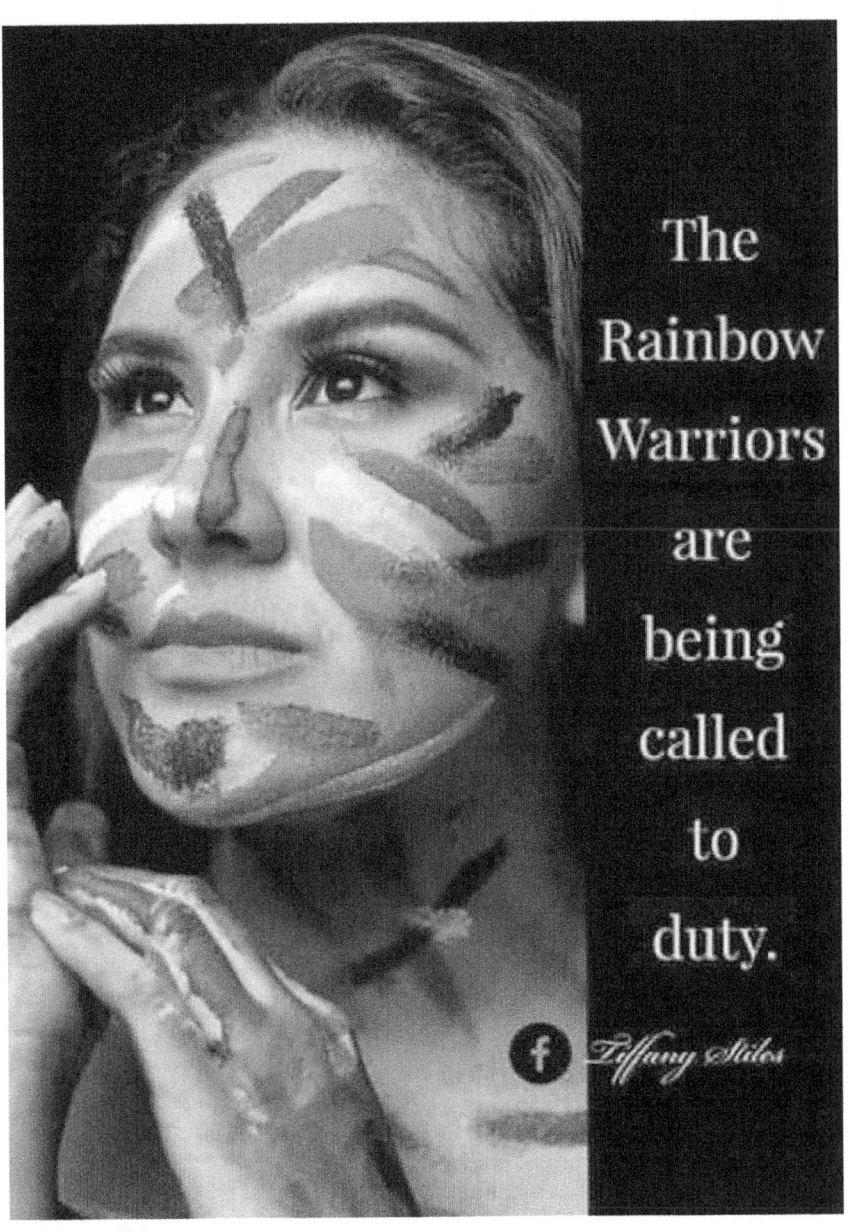

The Rainbow Warriors are being called to duty.

Tiffany Stiles

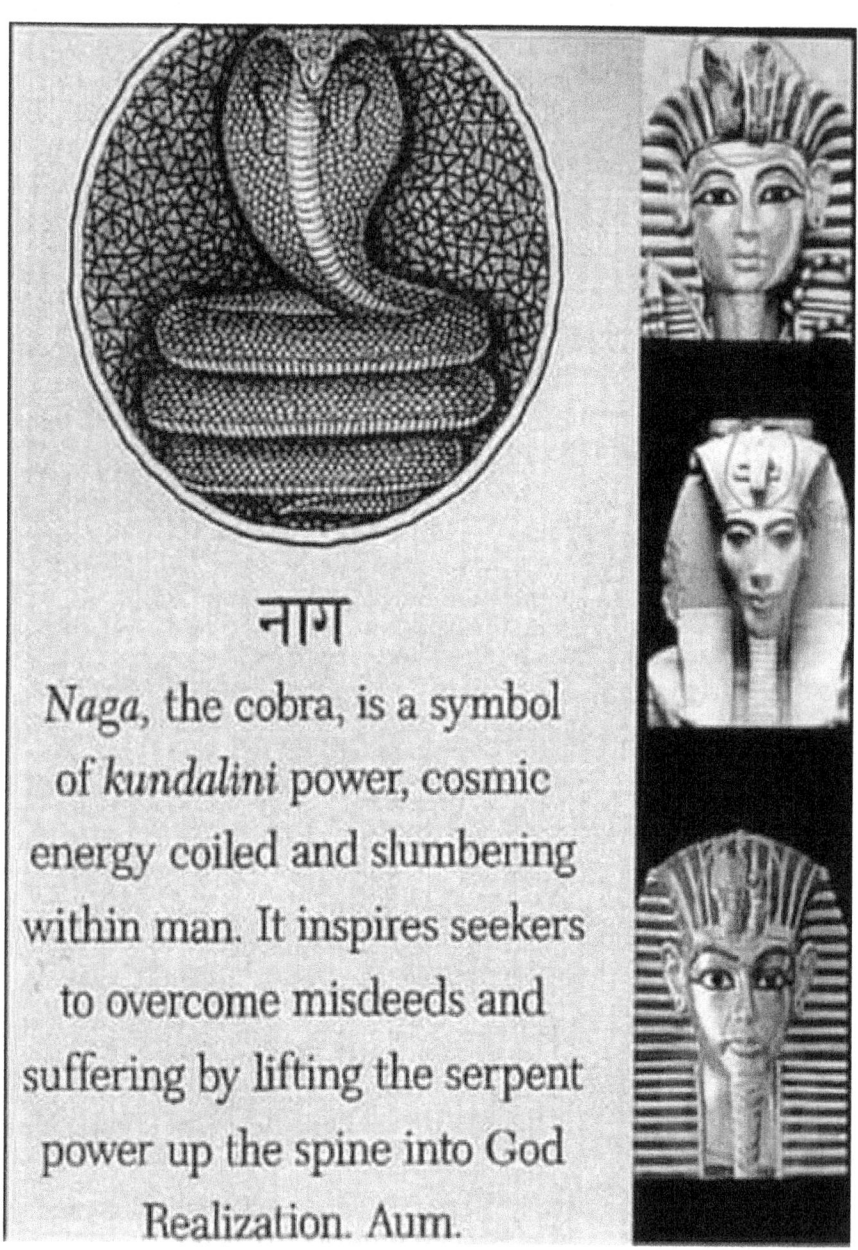

नाग

Naga, the cobra, is a symbol
of *kundalini* power, cosmic
energy coiled and slumbering
within man. It inspires seekers
to overcome misdeeds and
suffering by lifting the serpent
power up the spine into God
Realization. Aum.

The Egyptians placed the snake on the forehead to symbolize that they had awakened their own Kundalini Energy. It was placed on the head to show it had risen all the way up the spine and out of the third eye. Thus making them keeper of Knowledge. This single accomplishment had changed their entire being down to DNA and cellular levels..once this was done they no longer considered themselves human. They were now Gods

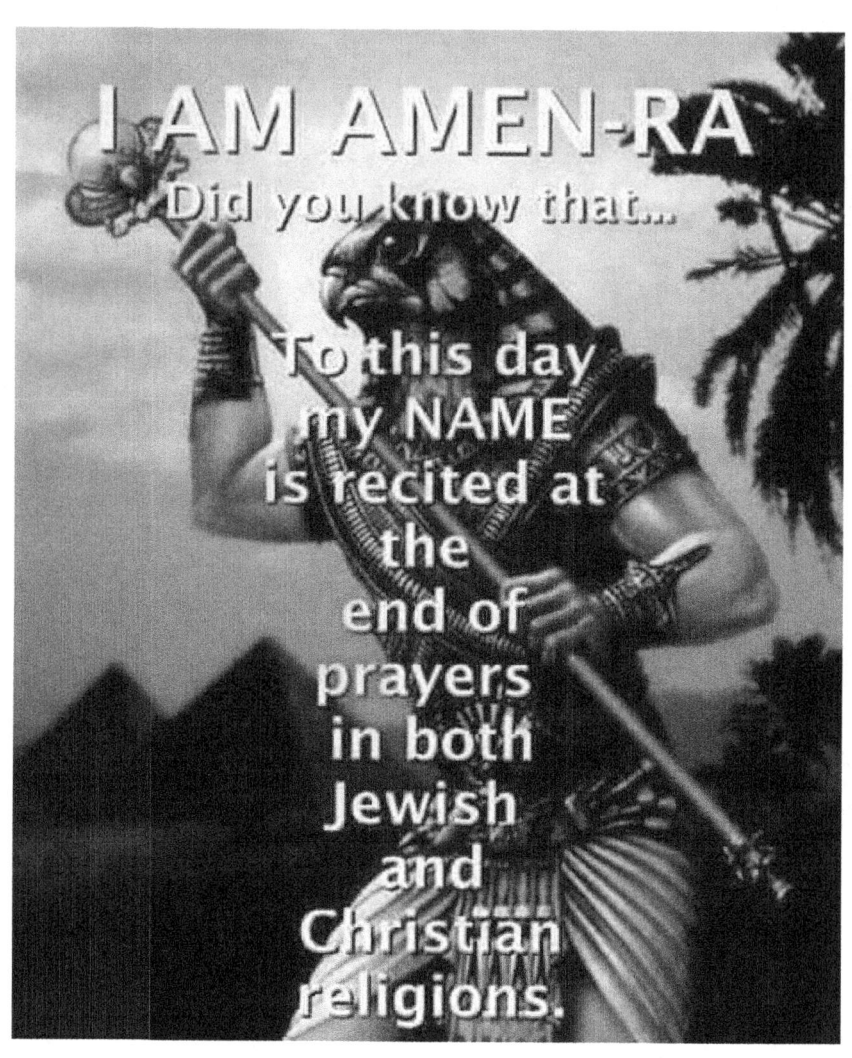

I AM AMEN-RA
Did you know that...

To this day
my NAME
is recited at
the
end of
prayers
in both
Jewish
and
Christian
religions.

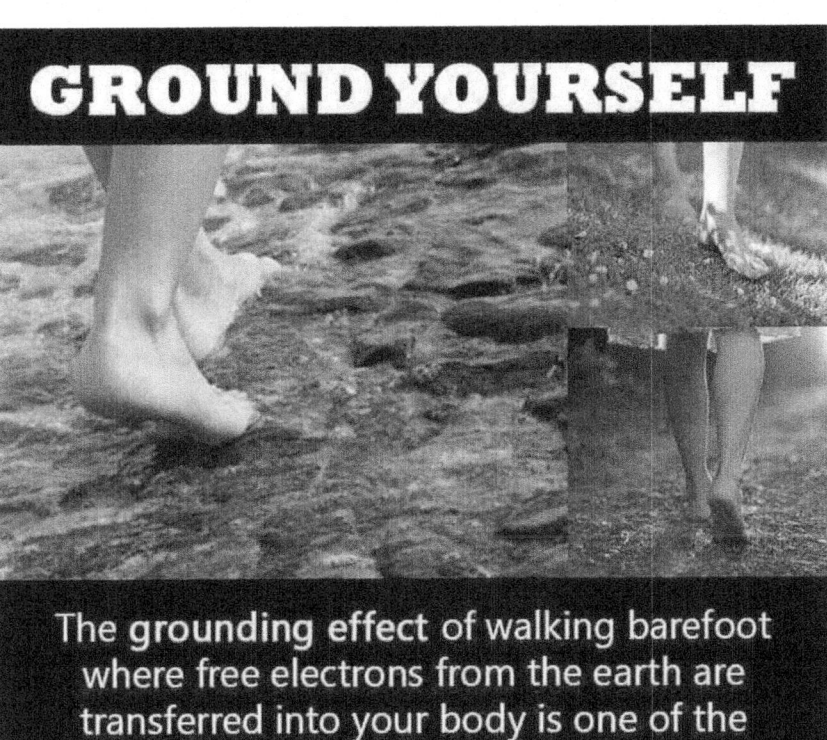

GROUND YOURSELF

The **grounding effect** of walking barefoot where free electrons from the earth are transferred into your body is one of the most **potent antioxidants** known in research.

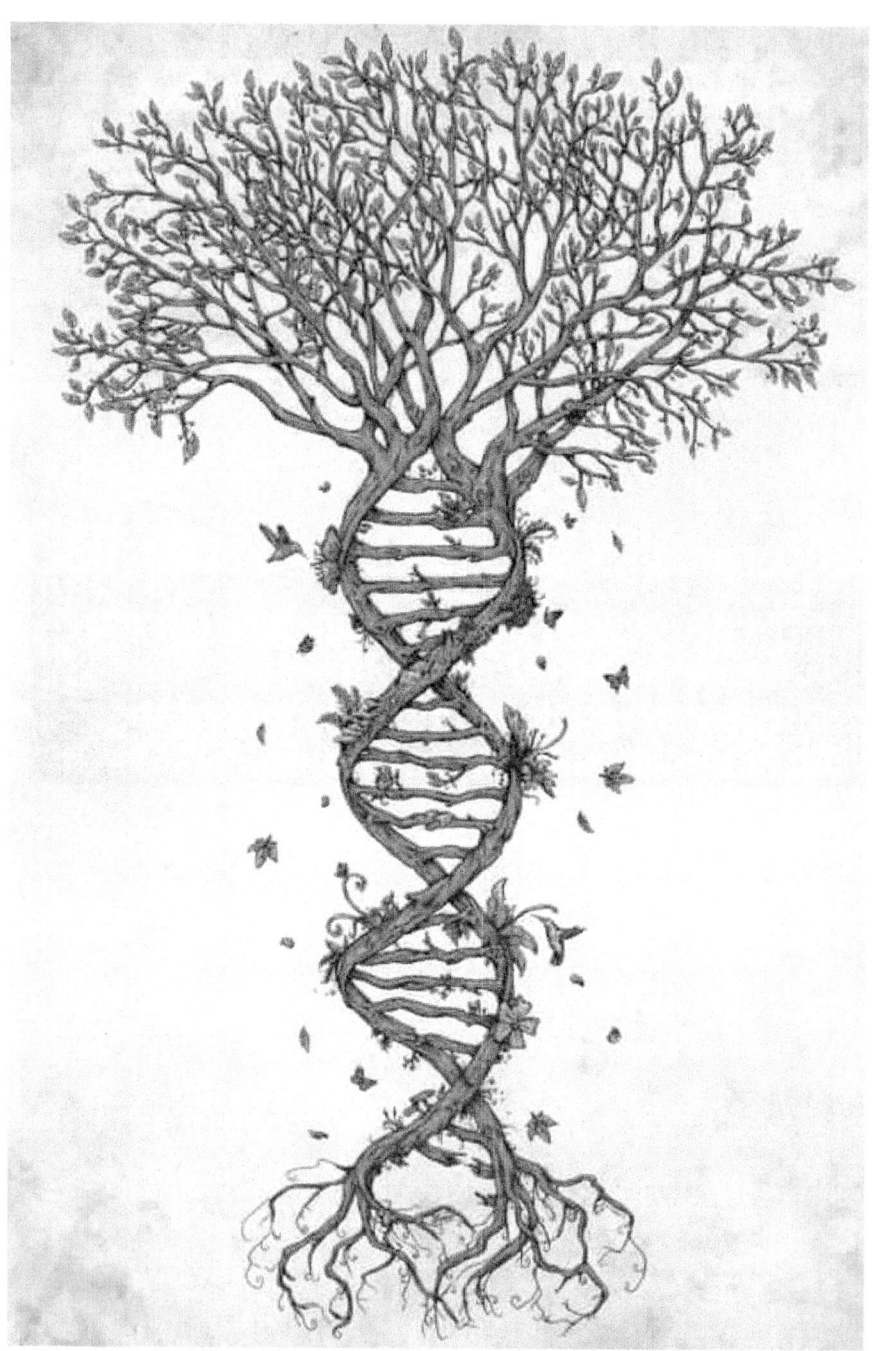

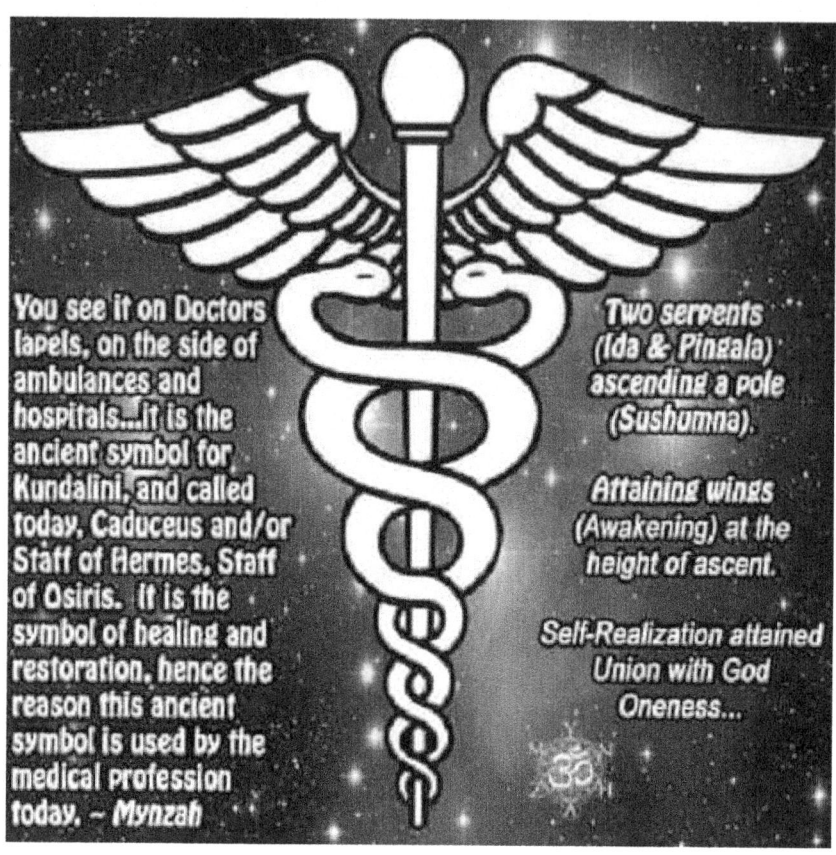

You see it on Doctors lapels, on the side of ambulances and hospitals...it is the ancient symbol for Kundalini, and called today, Caduceus and/or Staff of Hermes, Staff of Osiris. It is the symbol of healing and restoration, hence the reason this ancient symbol is used by the medical profession today. ~ Mynzah

Two serpents (Ida & Pingala) ascending a pole (Sushumna).

Attaining wings (Awakening) at the height of ascent.

Self-Realization attained Union with God Oneness...

164

DON'T LOSE YOUR CONNECTION WITH THE GREAT SPIRIT OVER THE WORDS IN A BOOK. THE CREATOR CAME FROM THE STARS AND OUR MESSAGE STRAIGHT FROM THE SOURCE.

From the music you love to listen to the art that entices you.From tiny flowers you see in your backyard to huge galaxies out there in Space & surprisingly your DNA follows it too. Ladies and Gentlemen the 'Golden Ratio'.

THERE ARE SEVEN ENERGY POINTS IN THE BODY KNOWN AS CHAKRAS, AND THERE ARE SEVEN MUSICAL NOTES IN THE CHROMATIC SCALE.

IG:@HEALINGFACTS

THIS IS NO COINCIDENCE.
MUSIC IS FREQUENCIES THAT AFFECT OUR ENERGY BODY AND OUR SUBCONSCIOUS MIND. BE AWARE OF WHAT YOU ARE LISTENING TO.

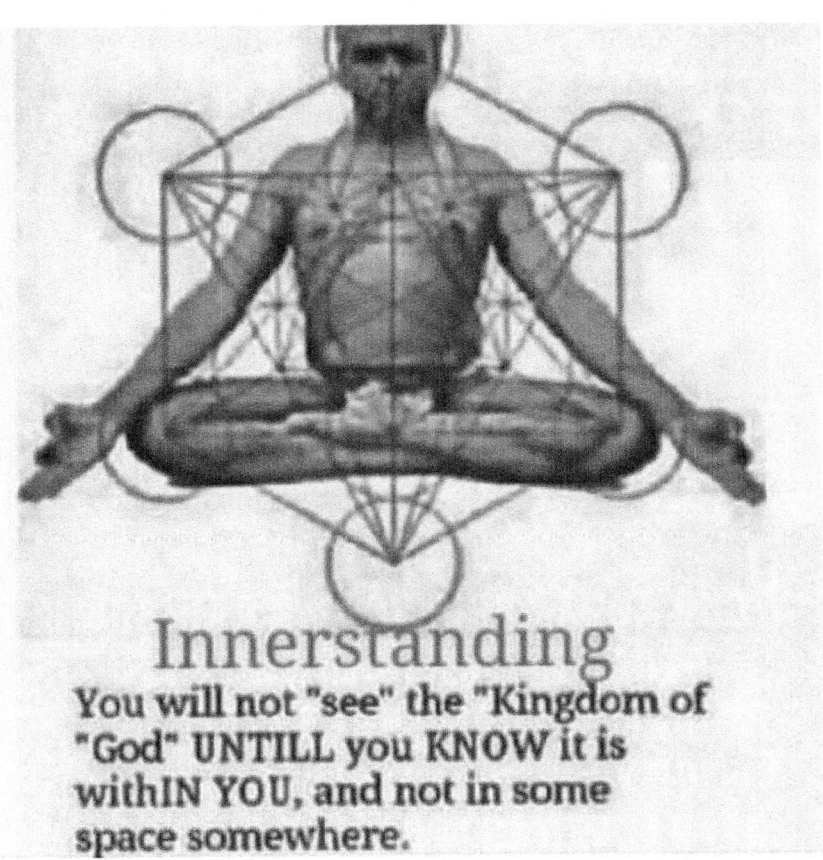

Innerstanding

You will not "see" the "Kingdom of "God" UNTILL you KNOW it is withIN YOU, and not in some space somewhere.

RAINBOW BODY

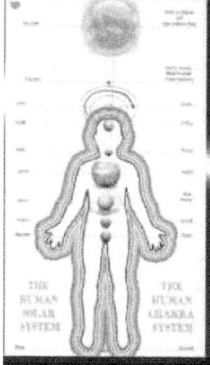  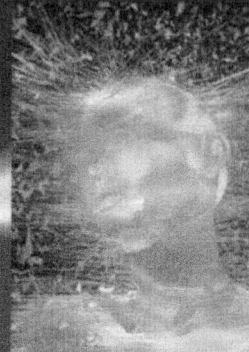

prism

@HolisticMedicine4u

YOUR AURA APPEARS AS A RAINBOW BECAUSE THE LIGHT WHICH IS EMINATING FROM THE CENTRAL SUN OF YOUR QUANTUM HEART IS REFRACTED AS IT PASSES THROUGH YOUR H2O RICH ORGANS AND CELLS. YOU ARE LITERALLY A RAINBOW IN CONSTANT CREATION

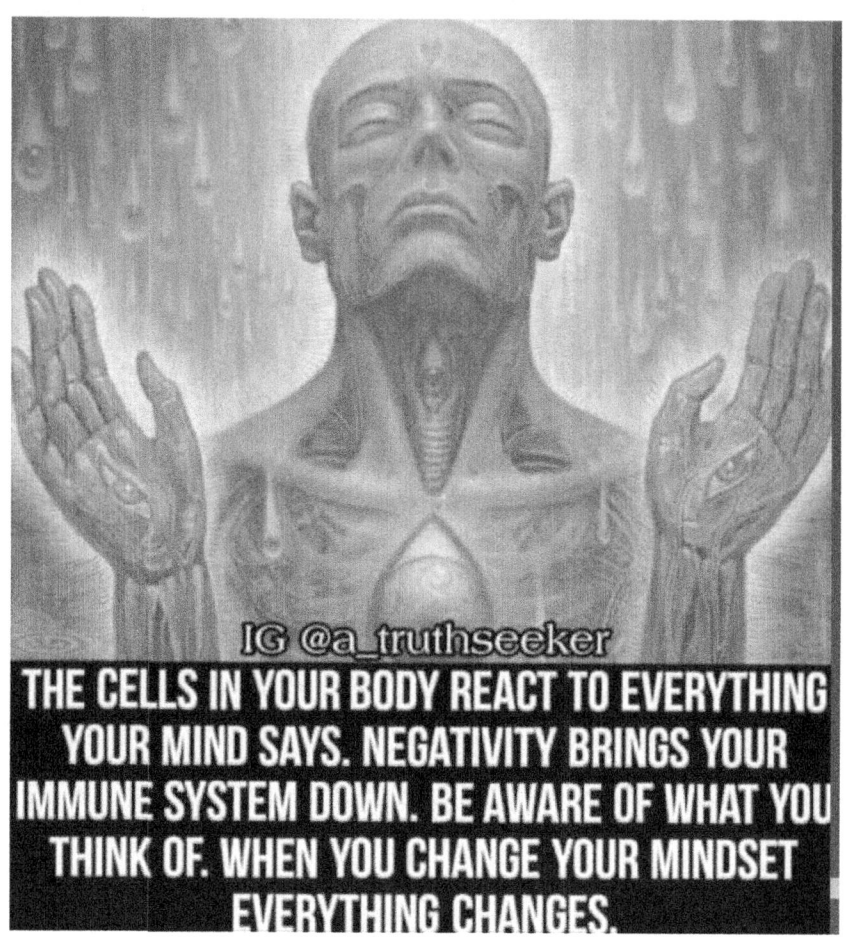

IG @a_truthseeker

THE CELLS IN YOUR BODY REACT TO EVERYTHING YOUR MIND SAYS. NEGATIVITY BRINGS YOUR IMMUNE SYSTEM DOWN. BE AWARE OF WHAT YOU THINK OF. WHEN YOU CHANGE YOUR MINDSET EVERYTHING CHANGES.

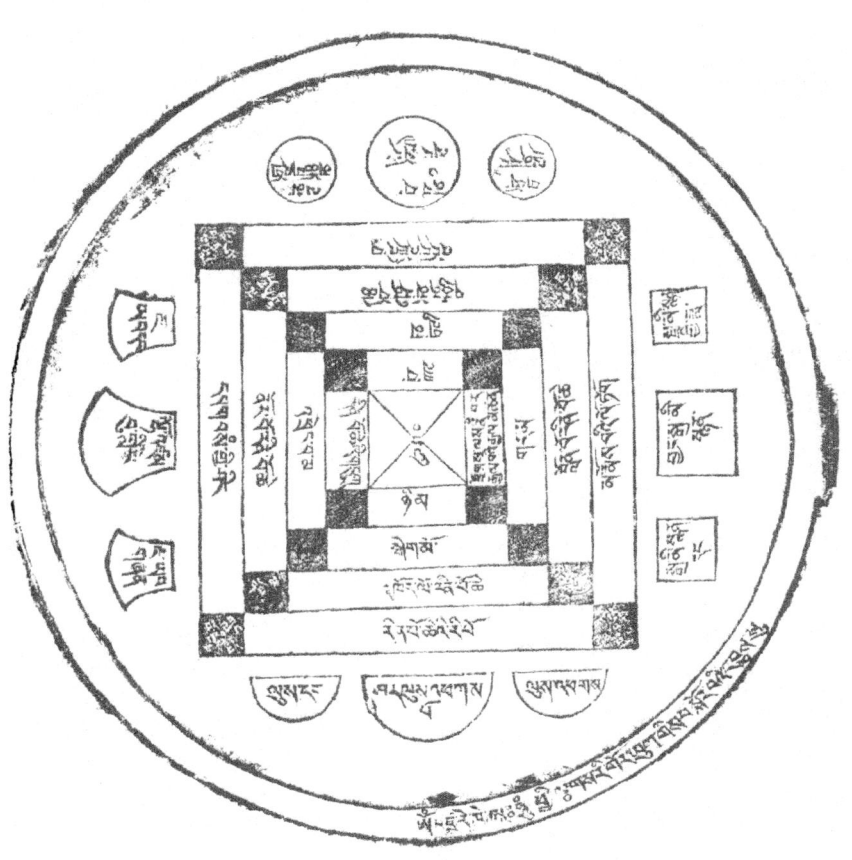

The Search for Truth

ChildrenofLight

Once you recognize the fact that the truth is not taught to the masses, the pursuit of truth can lead you into a path of solitude. The weak are constantly dependent on each other. Few have the strength to walk alone.

THE DARKNESS AND LIGHT BALANCE OF MIGHT

These months still have the Latin numbers in their names:

SEPtember 7th
OCTober 8th
NOVember 9th
DECember 10th

So, If DECember is the 10th month, let's continue

JANUARY 11th
FEBRUARY 12th
MARCH (Month the NEW YEAR BEGINS)

January 1st isn't the new year.

Living your naked
truth will always
disturb those living
well dressed lies.

The dark does not destroy the light; it defines it. It is our fear of the dark that casts our joy into the shadows.

The Map of Money Consciousness™

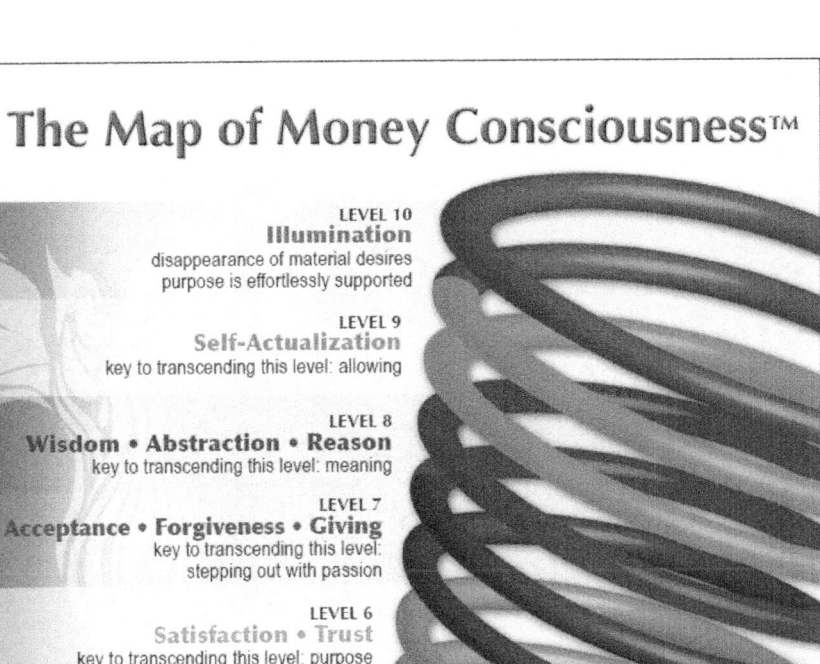

LEVEL 10
Illumination
disappearance of material desires
purpose is effortlessly supported

LEVEL 9
Self-Actualization
key to transcending this level: allowing

LEVEL 8
Wisdom • Abstraction • Reason
key to transcending this level: meaning

LEVEL 7
Acceptance • Forgiveness • Giving
key to transcending this level:
stepping out with passion

LEVEL 6
Satisfaction • Trust
key to transcending this level: purpose

LEVEL 5
Courage • Optimism
key to transcending this level: appreciation

LEVEL 4
Anger • Aggression
key to transcending this level:
use energy positively

LEVEL 3
Desire • Craving
key to transcending this level: I am worthy

LEVEL 2
Fear • Anxiety
key to transcending this level:
overcome fear

LEVEL 1
Blame • Despair • Apathy
key to transcending this level: take action

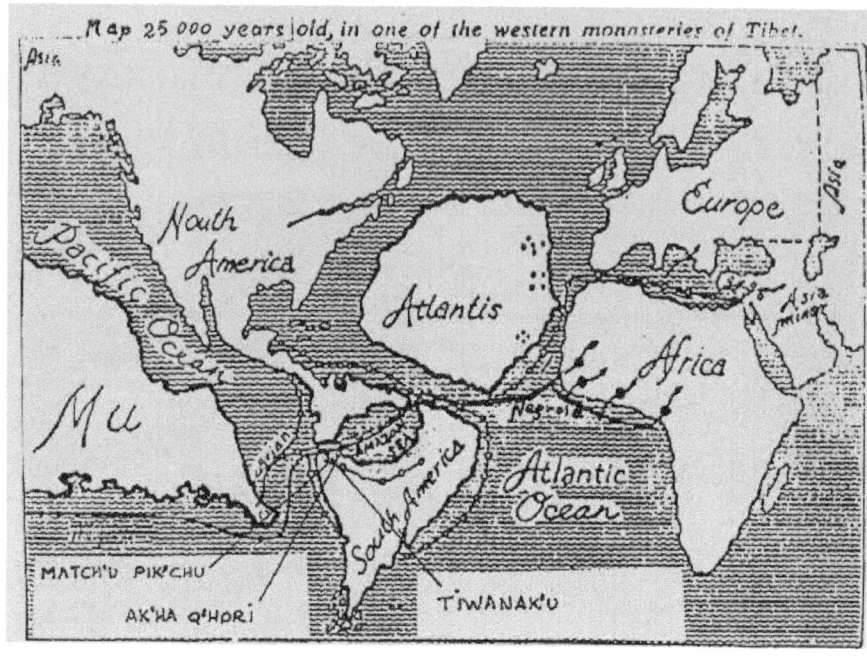

Map 25 000 years old, in one of the western monasteries of Tibet.

Noah's Ark

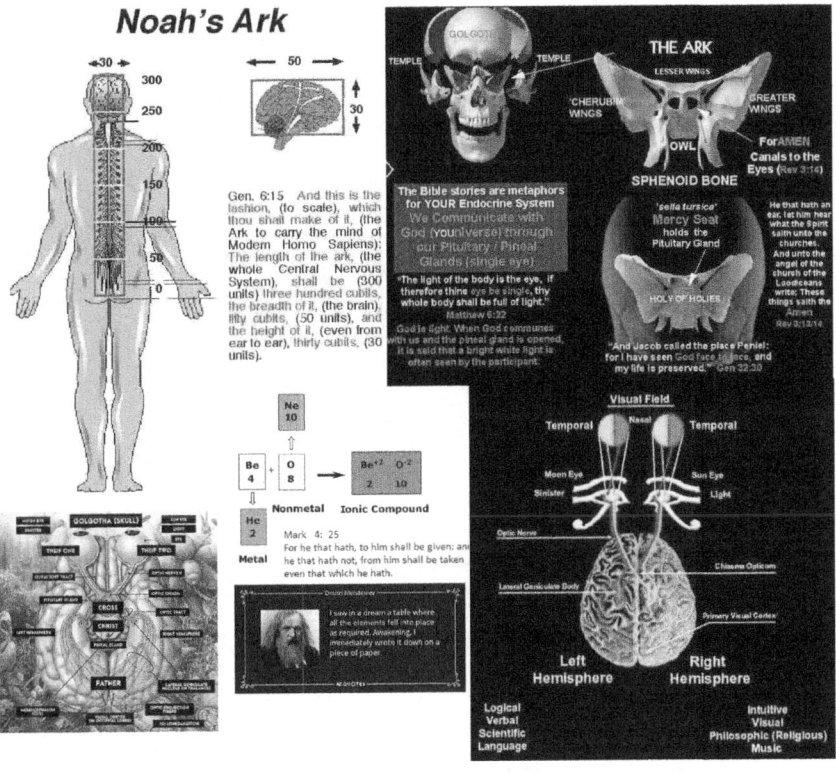

Gen. 6:15 And this is the fashion, (to scale), which thou shalt make of it, (the Ark to carry the mind of Modern Homo Sapiens): The length of the ark, (the whole Central Nervous System), shall be (300 units) three hundred cubits, the breadth of it, (the brain), fifty cubits, (50 units), and the height of it, (even from ear to ear), thirty cubits, (30 units).

The Bible stories are metaphors for YOUR Endocrine System
We Communicate with God (youniverse) through our Pituitary / Pineal Glands (single eye)

"The light of the body is the eye, if therefore thine eye be single, thy whole body shall be full of light." Matthew 6:32

God is light. When God communes with us and the pineal gland is opened, it is said that a bright white light is often seen by the participant.

THE ARK
LESSER WINGS
GREATER WINGS
'CHERUBIM' WINGS
OWL
SPHENOID BONE
For AMEN Canals to the Eyes (Rev 3:14)

'sella tursica'
Mercy Seat holds the Pituitary Gland

HOLY OF HOLIES

He that hath an ear, let him hear what the Spirit saith unto the churches. And unto the angel of the church of the Laodiceans write; These things saith the Amen Rev 3:13,14

"And Jacob called the place Peniel: for I have seen God face to face, and my life is preserved." Gen 32:30

Ne 10

Be 4 + O 8 → Be⁺² 2 O⁻² 10

Nonmetal   Ionic Compound

He 2

Metal

Mark 4: 25
For he that hath, to him shall be given: and he that hath not, from him shall be taken even that which he hath.

I saw in a dream a table where all the elements fell into place as required. Awakening, I immediately wrote it down on a piece of paper.

Visual Field
Temporal   Nasal   Temporal
Moon Eye   Sun Eye
Sinister   Light
Optic Nerve
Chiasma Opticum
Lateral Geniculate Body
Primary Visual Cortex

Left Hemisphere
Logical
Verbal
Scientific
Language

Right Hemisphere
Intuitive
Visual
Philosophic (Religious)
Music

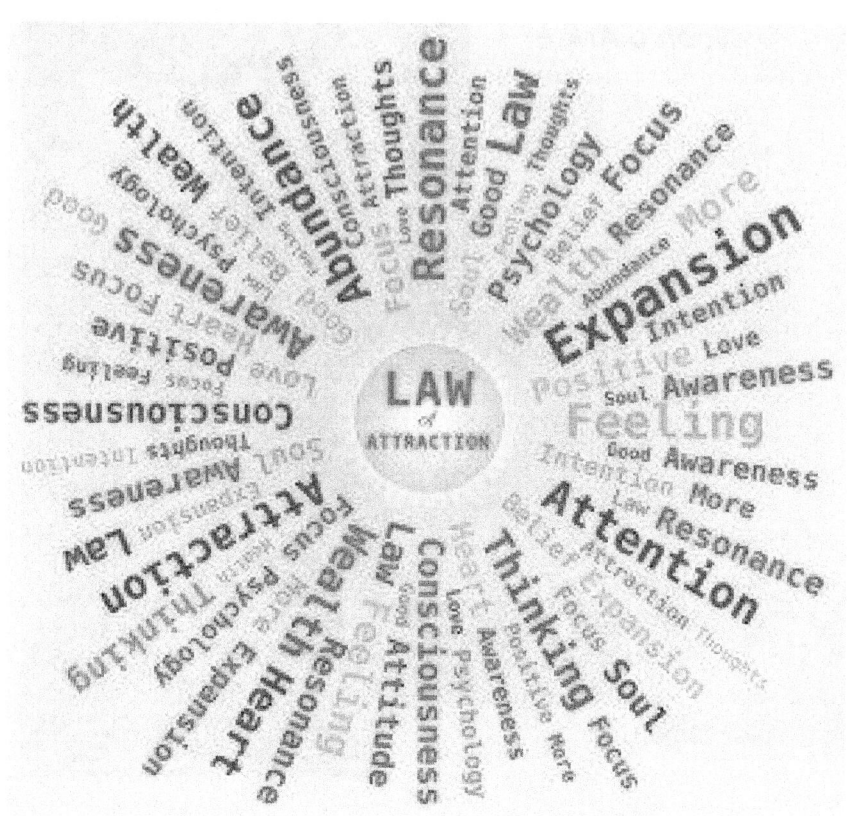

YOU ARE NO LONGER
STARSEEDS

Beloved one, this is a magnificent time for you because you are now blossoming into what you were always meant to become since the initiation of Mission Gaia.

You are now a Star-blossom. You are now ready to allow for the radiance of your true nature of unconditional love to flourish and bloom by means of your remembrance and re-connection to your cosmic roots.

You are now ready to embrace who you truly are, you've brought all of it along with you and you're now coming online to your multidimensionality with no need to change or upgrade your personality. And so it is, New Earth Now.

@Younification
Reconnecting the Family of Light

185

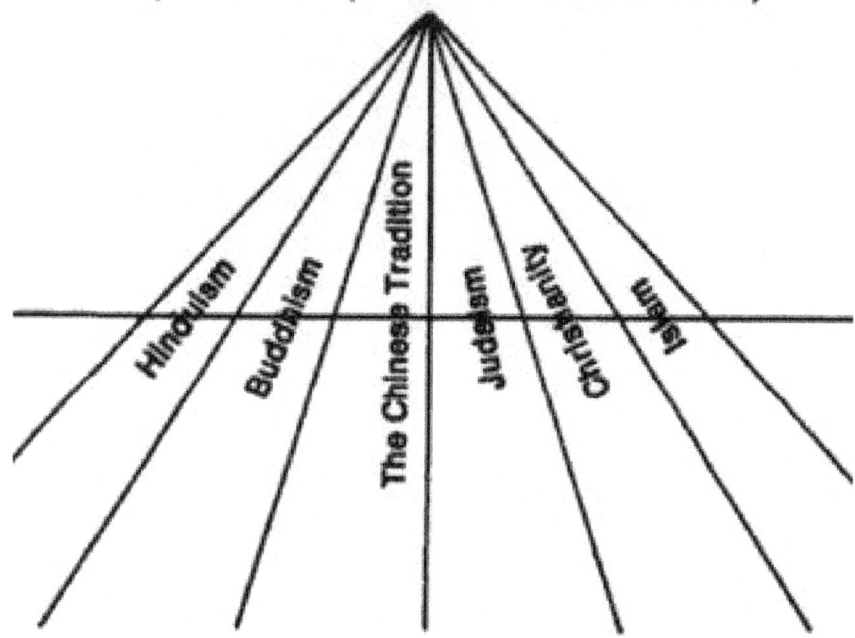

NONDUAL UNIVERSAL MINDNATURE OF 'GC
(Realm of quantum wavefunction)

Hinduism • Buddhism • The Chinese Tradition • Judaism • Christianity • Islam

REALM OF EMBODIED DUALISTIC EXPERIEN(

Universal Model

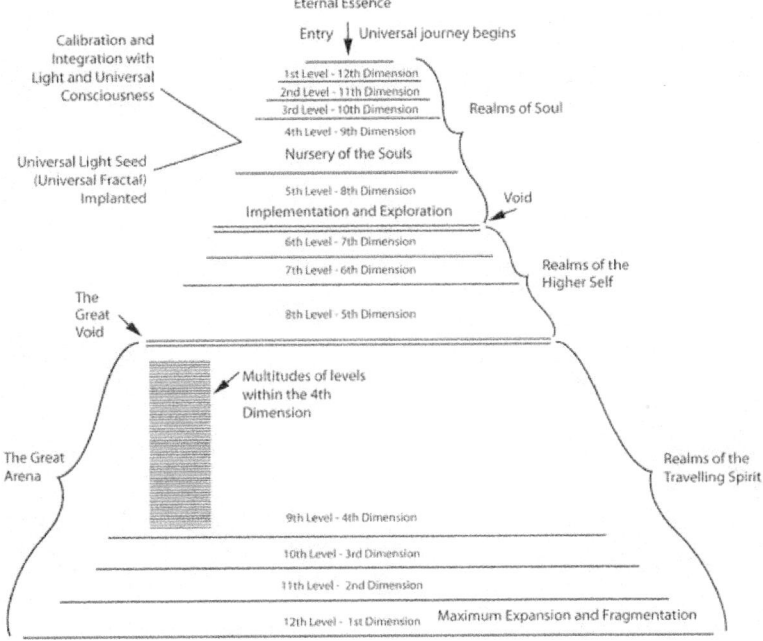

Eternal Essence

Entry | Universal journey begins

Calibration and Integration with Light and Universal Consciousness

1st Level - 12th Dimension
2nd Level - 11th Dimension
3rd Level - 10th Dimension — Realms of Soul
4th Level - 9th Dimension
Nursery of the Souls

Universal Light Seed (Universal Fractal) Implanted

5th Level - 8th Dimension — Void
Implementation and Exploration

6th Level - 7th Dimension
7th Level - 6th Dimension — Realms of the Higher Self

The Great Void

8th Level - 5th Dimension

Multitudes of levels within the 4th Dimension

The Great Arena

Realms of the Travelling Spirit

9th Level - 4th Dimension

10th Level - 3rd Dimension

11th Level - 2nd Dimension

12th Level - 1st Dimension   Maximum Expansion and Fragmentation

© www.ourjourneyhome.com.au

187

THE BLACK CUBE OF SATURN

DENMARK   MANHATTAN

—— GLOBAL OCCULT WORSHIP ——

KABBALAH INSPIRED SYMBOLS AND MEANING

When the Flower of Life is spinning, a coalescing pattern forms that is almost identical to the pole views of Saturn and Jupiter. Sacred geometry emanates from all spinning objects.

—Parinya Champ, 2009.

SATURN   JUPITER   FLOWER OF LIFE

Saturn/Jupiter Image Credit: NASA/JPL/GSFC/Oxford University

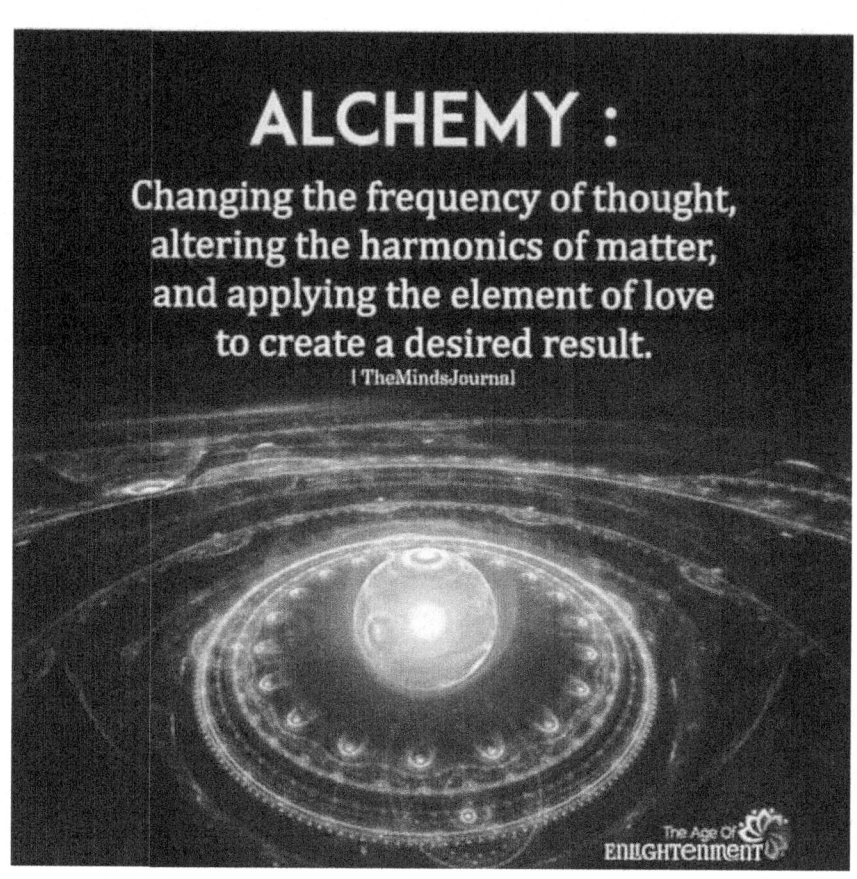

ALCHEMY :
Changing the frequency of thought,
altering the harmonics of matter,
and applying the element of love
to create a desired result.
[TheMindsJournal]

The Age Of
EnlIGHTenmenT

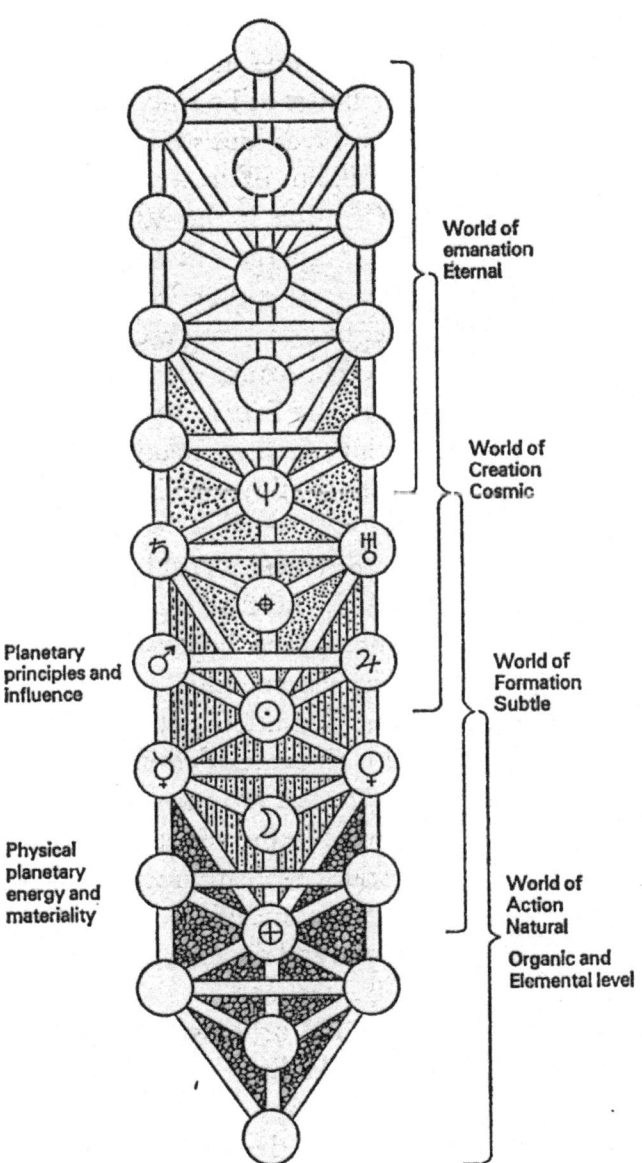

World of
emanation
Eternal

World of
Creation
Cosmic

Planetary
principles and
influence

World of
Formation
Subtle

Physical
planetary
energy and
materiality

World of
Action
Natural

Organic and
Elemental level

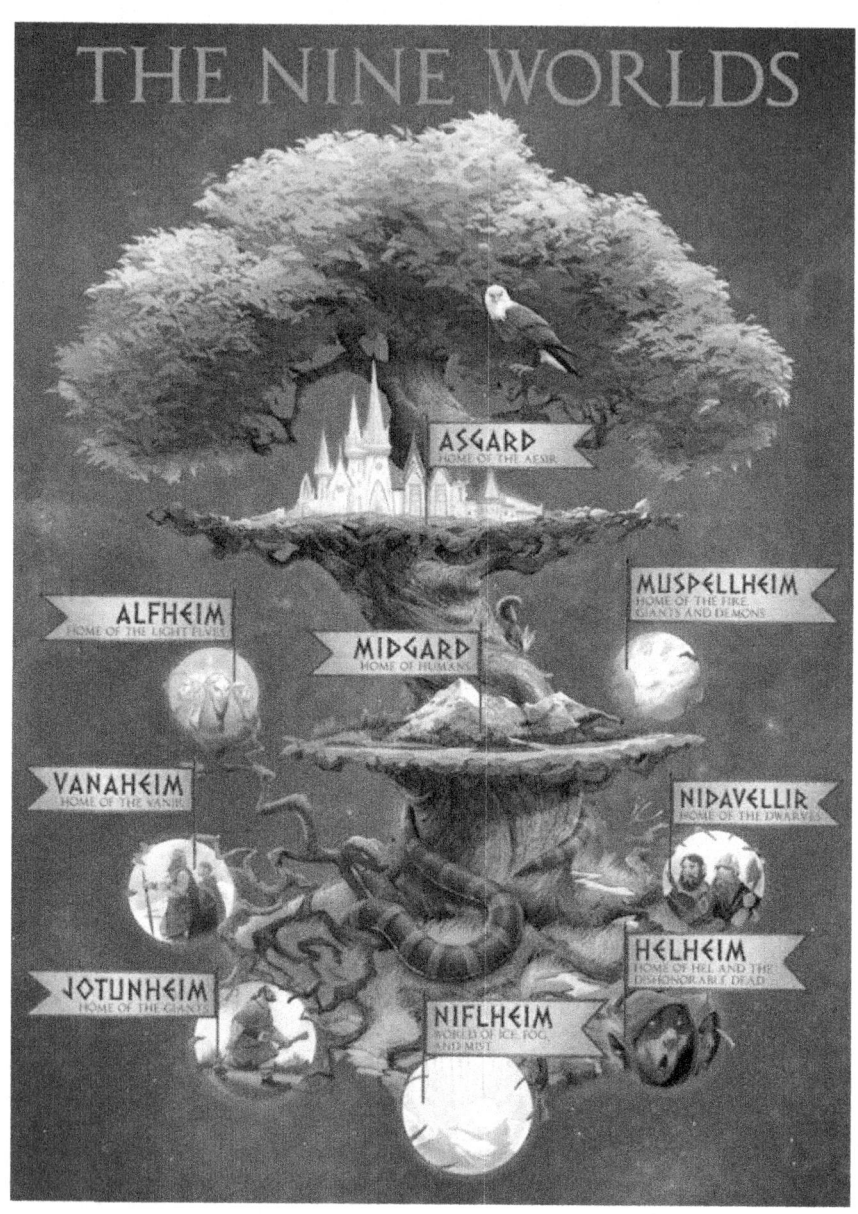

Some day, stories will be told about the soldiers of that time. Ordinary people who spent countless hours researching, debating, meditating and praying- and for the truth to continually be revealed to them.
Although they were mocked, dismissed and cast off, they knew their souls had agreed long ago to do this work.

I Am

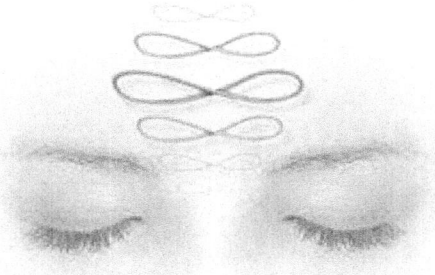

... the conscious embodiment
& Divine Presence
of unconditional Love
& of a 9th dimensional Flower of Life
working in me
& in every human being
in every moment
for the highest good of
ALL"

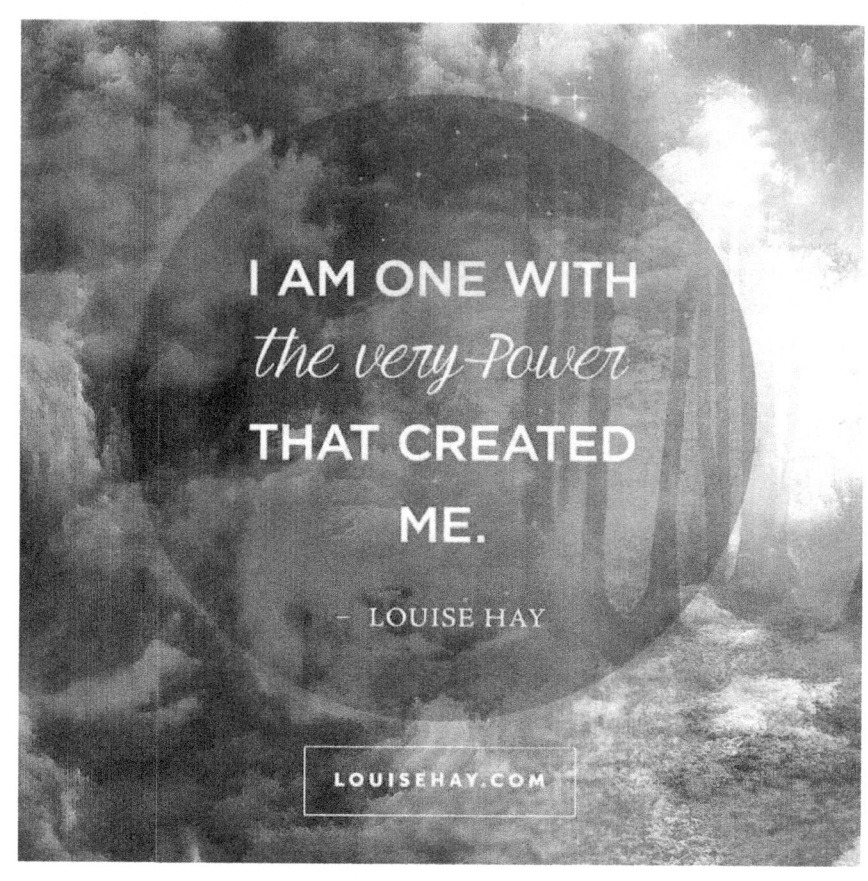

I AM ONE WITH
the very Power
THAT CREATED
ME.

– LOUISE HAY

LOUISEHAY.COM

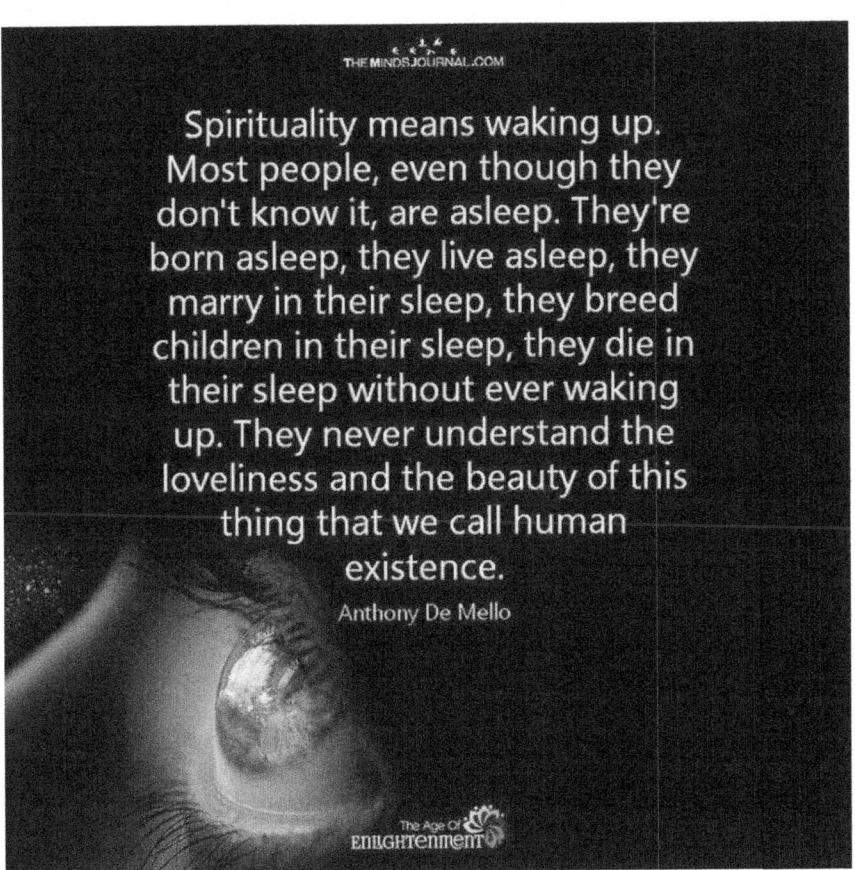

Spirituality means waking up. Most people, even though they don't know it, are asleep. They're born asleep, they live asleep, they marry in their sleep, they breed children in their sleep, they die in their sleep without ever waking up. They never understand the loveliness and the beauty of this thing that we call human existence.

Anthony De Mello

Bo·he·mi·an (n.)

\boh-hee-mee-uhn

1. A person, as an artist or writer, who lives and acts free of regard for conventional rules and practices

2. One who lives a wandering or vagabond life.

3. A free-spirited, open-minded thinker.

A wise man was once asked..
What is the meaning of life?

He replied..
Life itself has no meaning,
Life is an opportunity
to create meaning..

THE MIND UNLEASHED

	Ray	Color	Chakra	Archangels	Chohan	Elohim
1st	God Power / God Will / God MORE	Blue Ray	Throat	Archangel Michael and Faith	Master MORE (aka El Morya)	Elohim Hercules and Amazonia
2nd	Wisdom	Yellow Ray	Crown	Archangel Jophiel and Christine	Lord Lanto	Elohim Apollo and Lumina
3rd	Love	Pink Ray	Heart	Archangel Chamuel & Charity	Paul the Venetian	Elohim Heros and Amora
4th	Purity	White Ray	Base	Archangel Gabriel and Hope	Serapis Soleil (aka Serapis Bey)	God Purity and Elohim Astrea
5th	Healing / Truth / Music	Emerald Ray	Third Eye	Archangel Raphael and Mother Mary	Hilarion	Elohim Cyclopea and Virginia
6th	Peace	Purple Ray	Solar Plexus	Archangel Uriel and Aurora	Lady Master Nada	God Peace and Aloha
7th	Freedom	Violet Ray	Seat of the Soul / Sacral	Archangel Zadkiel and Amethyst	Saint Germain	Elohim Arturus and Victoria
8th	Integration	Ruby Ray	Secret Chamber of the Heart	Archangel Uzziel	Maha Chohan	
9th	Meditation / Enlightenment Ray	Light Violet	Vortex above crown		ISIS and OSIRIS	Elohim Marcus and Elizabeth
10th	Creation Ray	Turquoise	Hands		Chananda	God & Goddess of Freedom
11th	Oneness Ray	Peach	Feet	Archangel Micah		
12th	Now Ray	White with Silver Streaks	Aura			

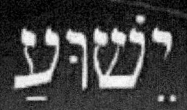

יְשׁוּעַ Joshua / Jeshua (Nehemiah)

YEH SHUA	
YEH SHUA	A DROPPED BECAUSE THERE IS NO GREEK CHARCTER FOR HEBREW AYIN
YEH SOU	SH DROPPED BECAUSE THERE IS NO GREEK CHARCTER FOR HEBREW SHIN
IE SOU	HEBREW YEH = GREEK IE HEBREW / GREEK EQUIVALENT
IE SOUS	S ADDED IN GREEK AS A NOMINATIVE CASE ENDING (INDICATING A NAME)
IE SUS	O DROPPED IN ENGLISH TRANSLITERATION AS FOUND IN THE ORIGINAL KING JAMES
JE SUS	J REPLACED I IN LATER ENGLISH KING JAMES VERSIONS

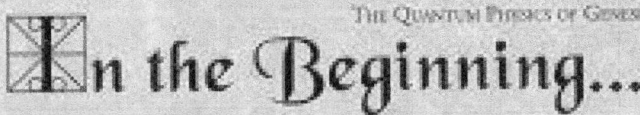

THE QUANTUM PHYSICS OF GENESIS

In the Beginning...

Start with One Proton Hydrogen

And Let There Be Light

Timespace

FreeWill

Universal Model showing
Synthetic Universe

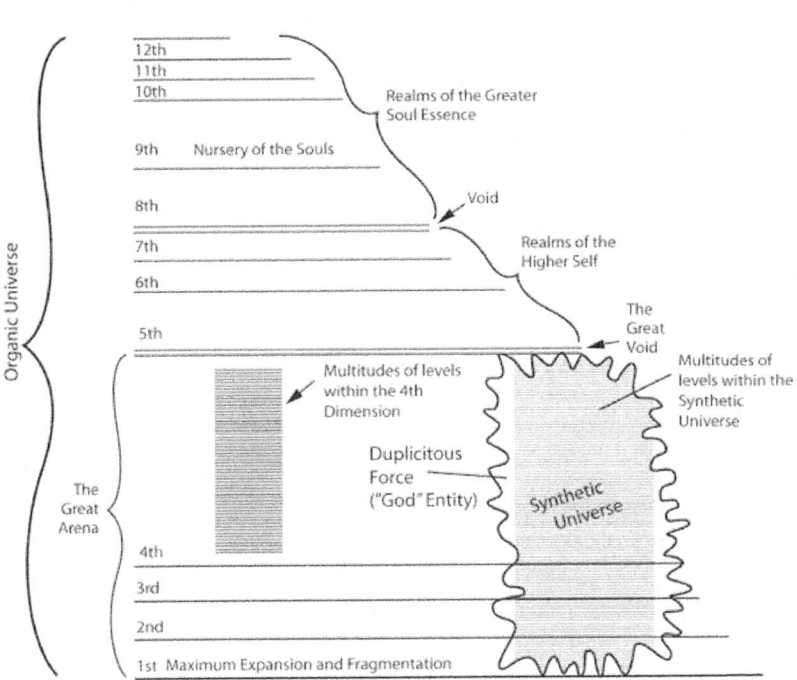

© **www.ourjourneyhome.com.au**

Hyos Ha Koidesh

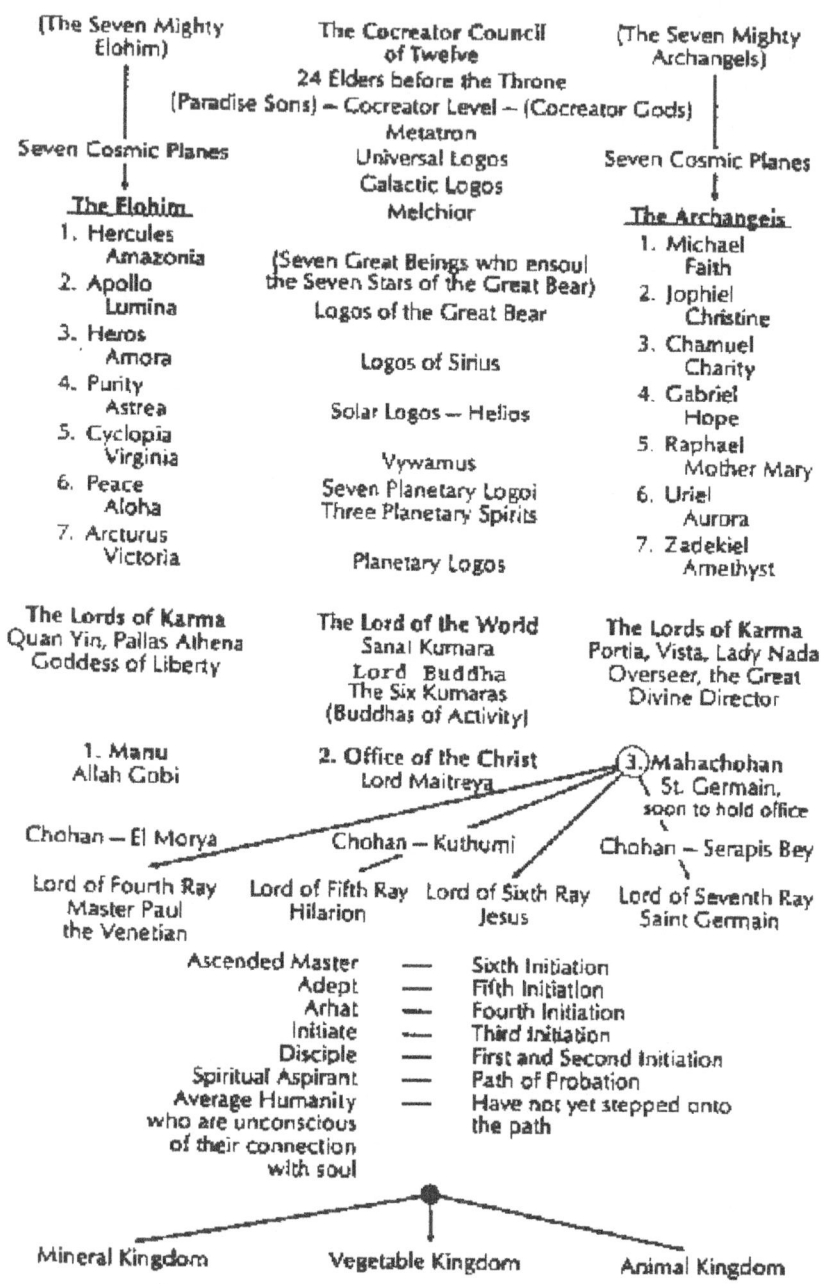

(The Seven Mighty Elohim)	The Cocreator Council of Twelve	(The Seven Mighty Archangels)
	24 Elders before the Throne	
	(Paradise Sons) — Cocreator Level — (Cocreator Gods)	
Seven Cosmic Planes	Metatron	Seven Cosmic Planes
	Universal Logos	
	Galactic Logos	
The Elohim	Melchior	**The Archangels**
1. Hercules Amazonia		1. Michael Faith
2. Apollo Lumina	(Seven Great Beings who ensoul the Seven Stars of the Great Bear)	2. Jophiel Christine
3. Heros Amora	Logos of the Great Bear	3. Chamuel Charity
4. Purity Astrea	Logos of Sirius	4. Gabriel Hope
5. Cyclopia Virginia	Solar Logos — Helios	5. Raphael Mother Mary
6. Peace Aloha	Vywamus Seven Planetary Logoi	6. Uriel Aurora
7. Arcturus Victoria	Three Planetary Spirits	7. Zadekiel Amethyst
	Planetary Logos	

The Lords of Karma Quan Yin, Pallas Athena Goddess of Liberty	The Lord of the World Sanal Kumara Lord Buddha The Six Kumaras (Buddhas of Activity)	The Lords of Karma Portia, Vista, Lady Nada Overseer, the Great Divine Director

1. Manu
Allah Gobi

2. Office of the Christ
Lord Maitreya

3. Mahachohan
St. Germain,
soon to hold office

Chohan — El Morya

Chohan — Kuthumi

Chohan — Serapis Bey

Lord of Fourth Ray
Master Paul
the Venetian

Lord of Fifth Ray
Hilarion

Lord of Sixth Ray
Jesus

Lord of Seventh Ray
Saint Germain

Ascended Master	—	Sixth Initiation
Adept	—	Fifth Initiation
Arhat	—	Fourth Initiation
Initiate	—	Third Initiation
Disciple	—	First and Second Initiation
Spiritual Aspirant	—	Path of Probation
Average Humanity who are unconscious of their connection with soul	—	Have not yet stepped onto the path

Mineral Kingdom   Vegetable Kingdom   Animal Kingdom

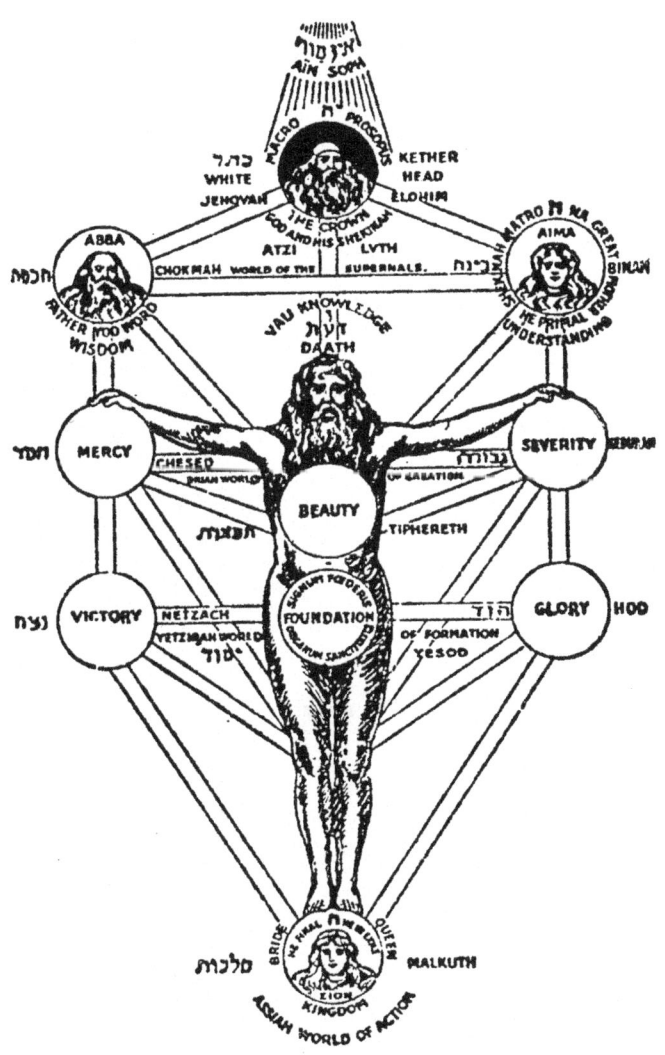

205

206

209

Hierarchy of the Soul

God Position

Highest Level of Abstraction

- Love of Truth - The highest goal and object worthy of greatest affection. Sacrifice everything for this

Reason, Humility
- Reason - the means of knowing while
- Humility - willing to be wrong and not willing to claim you have ever arrived at 100% certainty. There is always more you could know, so stay alert.

Life, Morality
- Choosing to live and recognizing the life depends on following the rules of this world and acting accordingly. Not all thoughts or actions correlate with a successful life

Integrity, Honesty, Justice
- Primary Values that enable one to best pursue morality, exercise reason, and discover the truth

Courage, Discipline
- Secondary Values that are needed to obtain the primary values

Respect, Independence
- Recognizing that the responsibility of judgment is personal and should be accepted personally and respected publically

Productiveness and Competence
- The process of creating order out of chaos through word and deed

Compassion
- Recognizing limitations in oneself and others. Choosing to help oneself and others overcome shortcomings in the pursuit of truth

Specific Judgments and Actions
- All judged by the hierarchy above

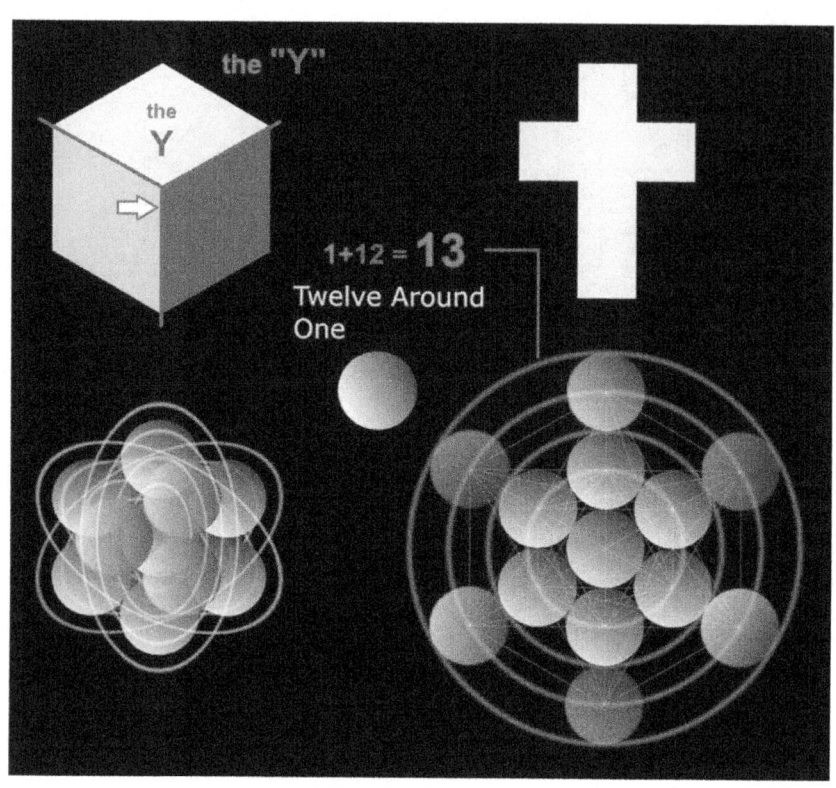

Right eye
(Eye of Ra)

Left eye
(Eye of Horus)

Related to the sun

Related to the moon

213

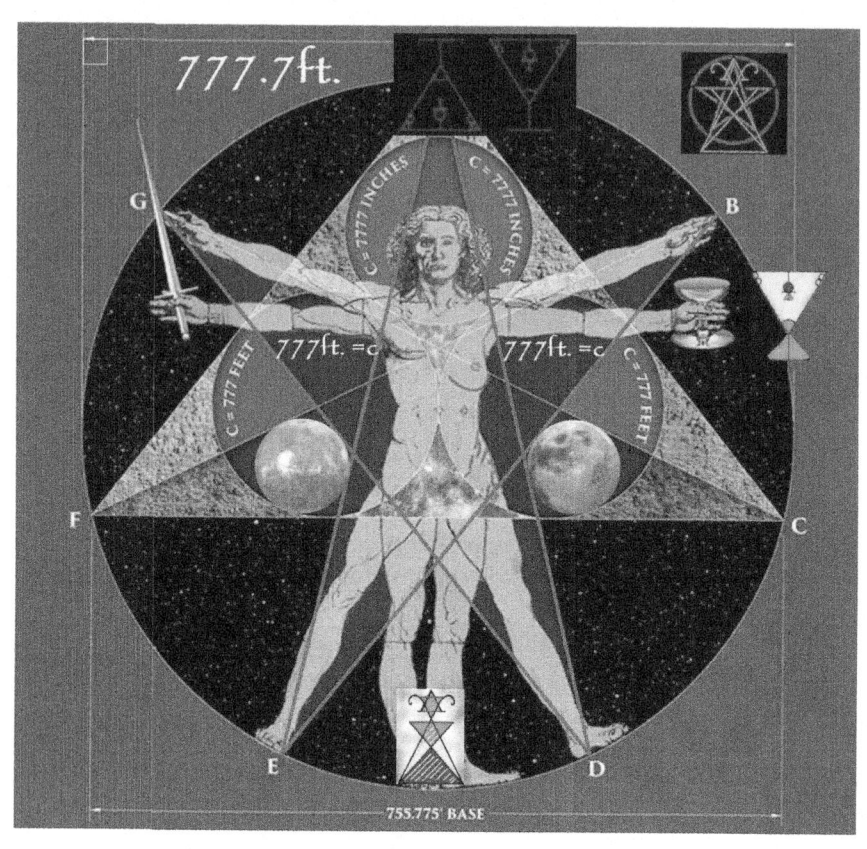

777.7ft.

755.775' BASE

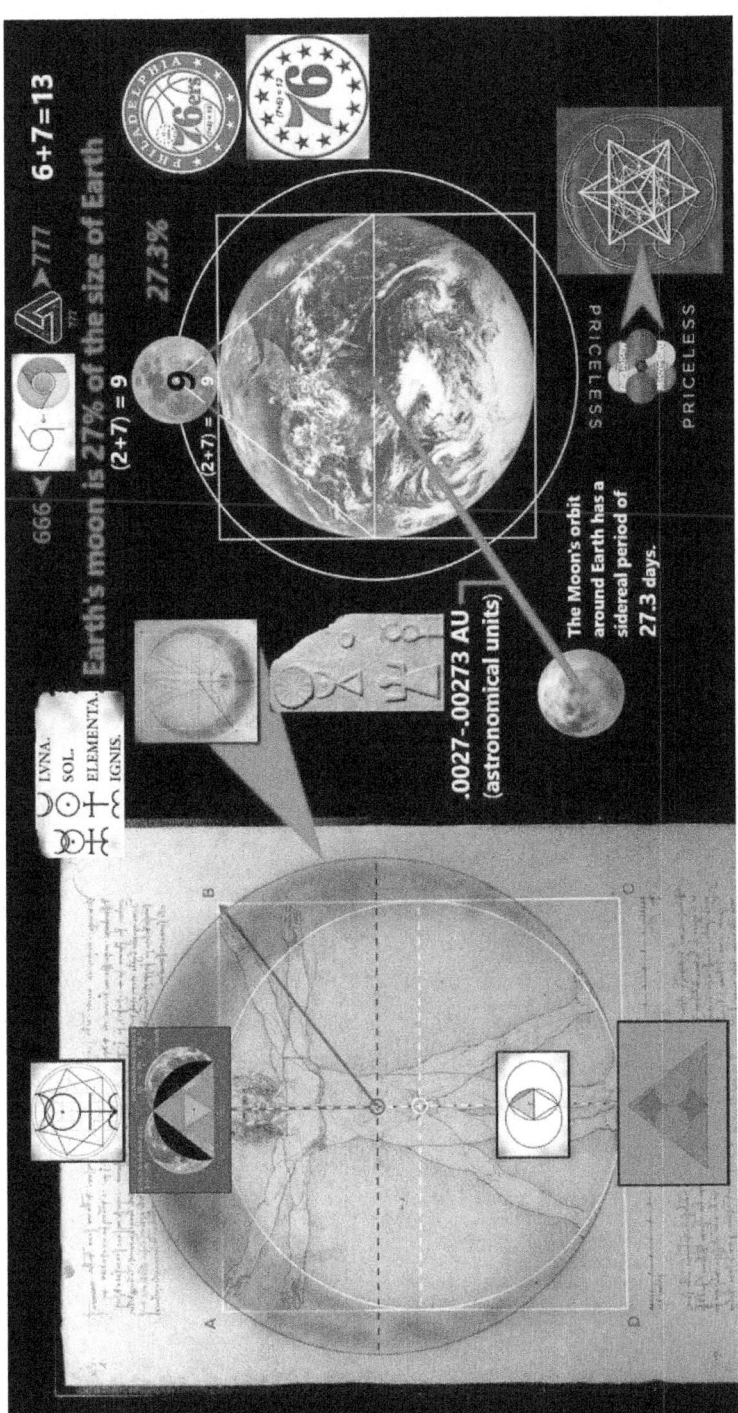

666 ➤ 777 6+7=13

Earth's moon is 27% of the size of Earth

(2+7) = 9

27.3%

(2+7) = 9

9

.0027-.00273 AU
(astronomical units)

The Moon's orbit
around Earth has a
sidereal period of
27.3 days.

PRICELESS

PRICELESS

LVNA.
SOL.
ELEMENTA.
IGNIS.

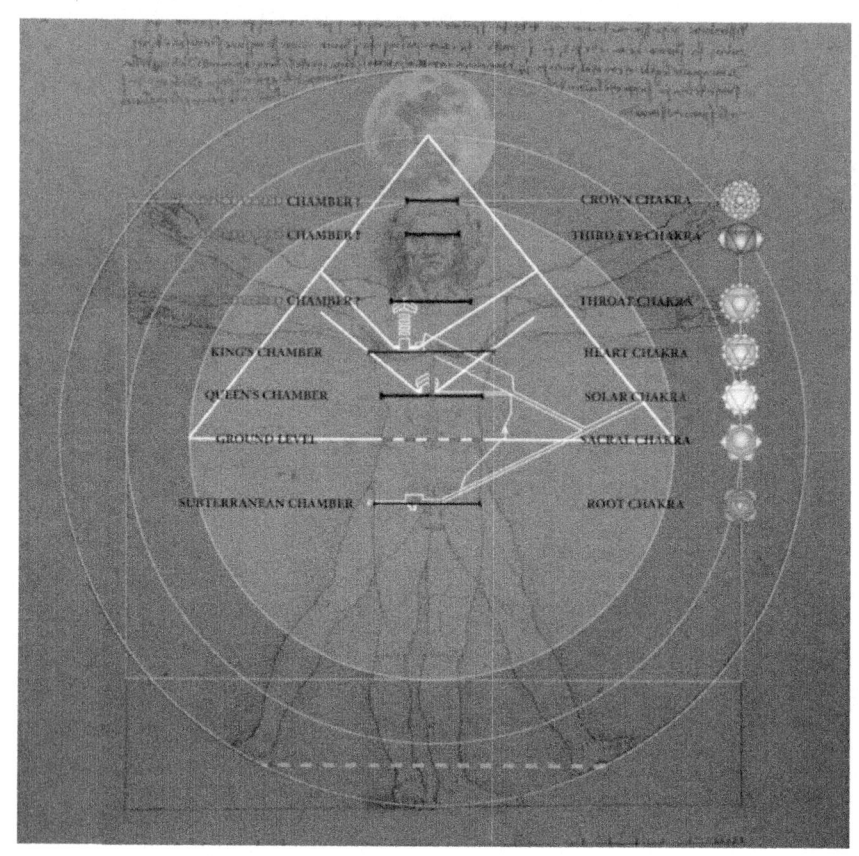

216

Sacred Geometry Shapes

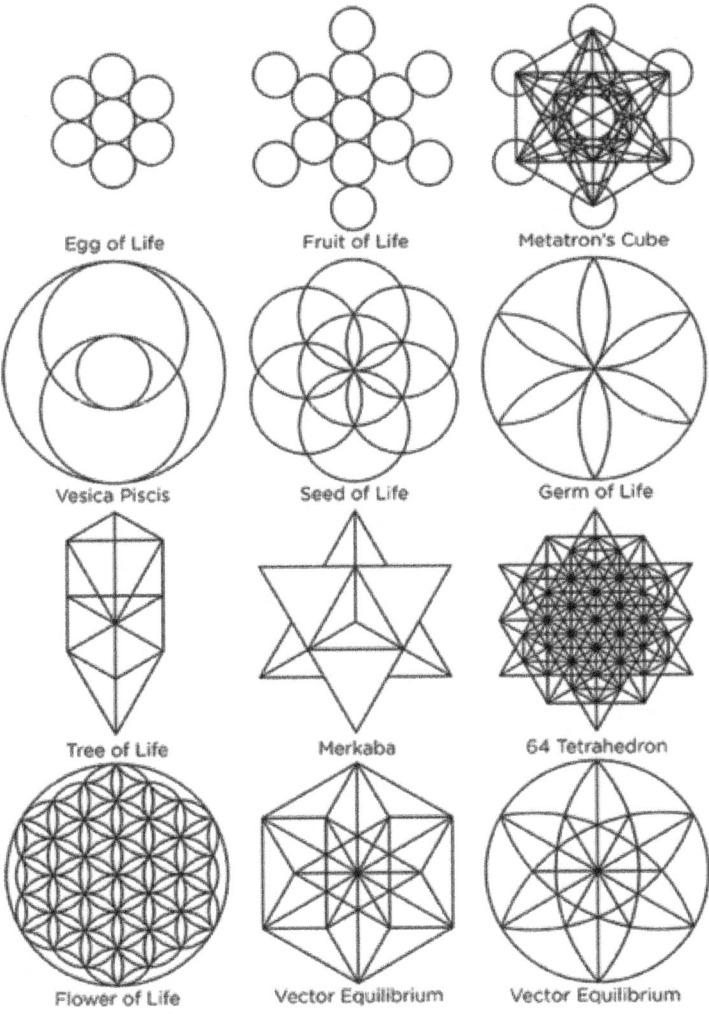

Egg of Life   Fruit of Life   Metatron's Cube

Vesica Piscis   Seed of Life   Germ of Life

Tree of Life   Merkaba   64 Tetrahedron

Flower of Life   Vector Equilibrium   Vector Equilibrium

THE SOLAR HIERARCHY
The Solar Logos.
|

The Solar Trinity or Logoi
I   The Father.......................Will.
II The Son.................Love-Wisdom.
III The Holy Spirit....Active Intelligence.
|

The Seven Rays
Three Rays of Aspect.
Four Rays of Attribute.
I. Will or Power....II. Love-Wisdom....III. Active Intelligence
|
4. Harmony or Beauty.
5. Concrete Knowledge.
6. Devotion or Idealism.
7. Ceremonial Magic

THE PLANETARY HIERARCHY
S. Sanat Kumara, the Lord of the World.
(The Ancient of Days.
The One Initiator).
|

The Three Kumaras.
(The Buddhas of Activity.)
1   2   3
|

The reflections of the 3 major and 4 minor Rays.

The 3 Departmental Heads.

I. *The Will Aspect*....... II. *The Love-Wisdom Aspect.* III. *Intelligence Aspect.*

A. The Manu.   B. The Bodhisattva.   C. The Mahachohan.
                 (The Christ.   (Lord of Civilisation)
                 The World Teacher.)

b. Master Jupiter.   b. A European Master.

c. Master M—.   c. Master K.H.   c. The Venetian Master.

                d. Master D.K.   4. The Master Serapis.
                               5. Master Hilarion.
                               6. Master Jesus.
                               7. Master R—.

Four grades of initiates.   Rakoczi

Various grades of disciples.

People on the Probationary Path.

Average humanity of all degrees.

WHAT YOU THINK, YOU BECOME.
WHAT YOU FEEL, YOU ATTRACT.
WHAT YOU IMAGINE, YOU CREATE.

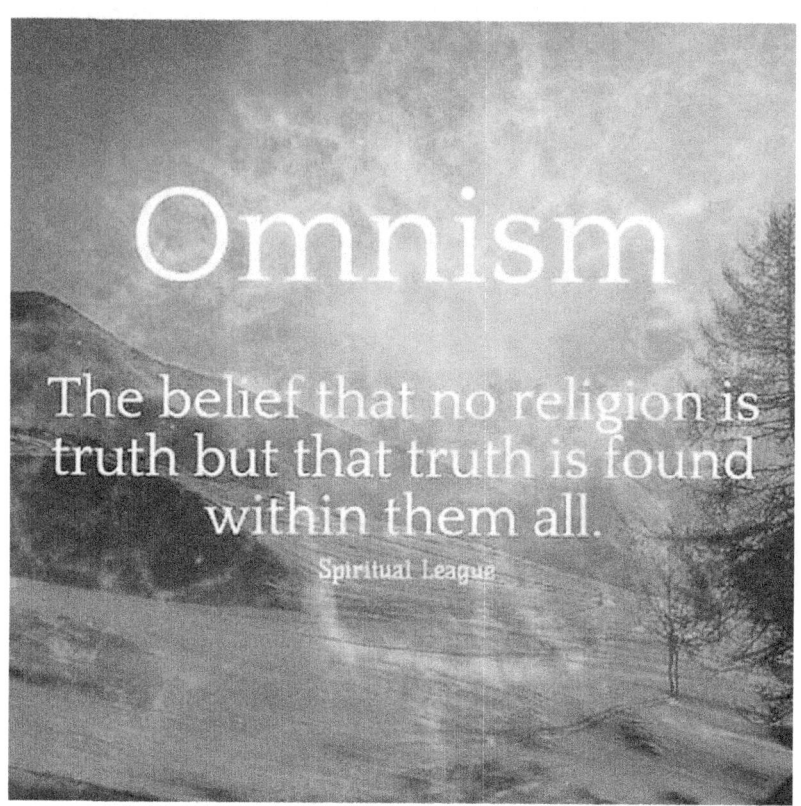

Omnism

The belief that no religion is truth but that truth is found within them all.

Spiritual League

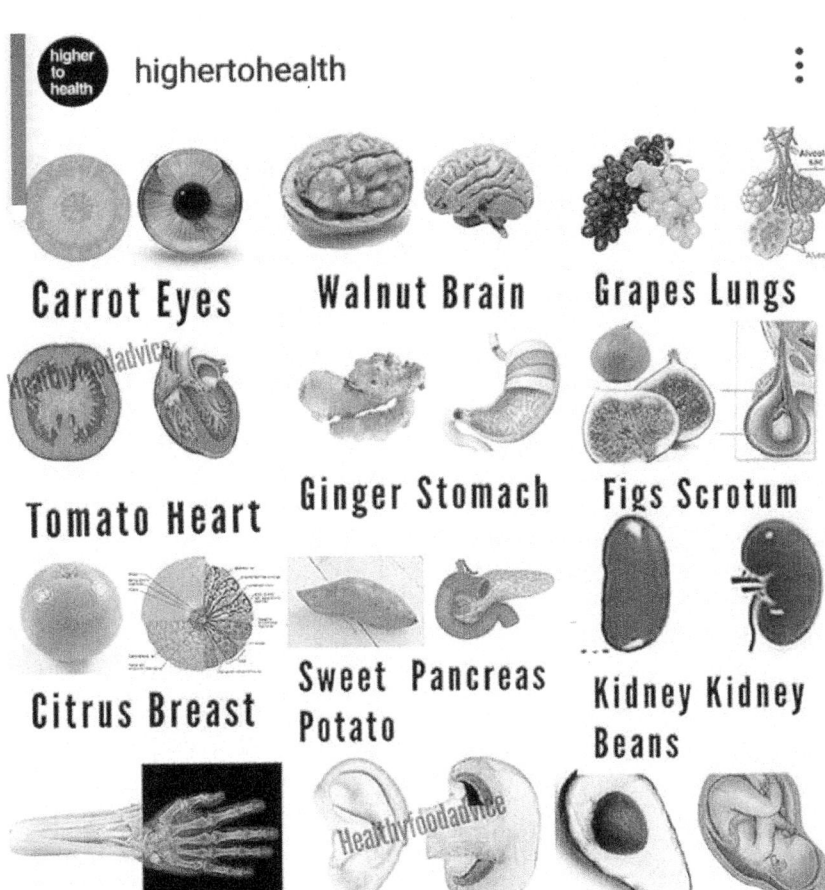

Carrot Eyes   Walnut Brain   Grapes Lungs

Tomato Heart   Ginger Stomach   Figs Scrotum

Citrus Breast   Sweet Pancreas Potato   Kidney Kidney Beans

Bones Celery   Hearing Mushroom   Avocado Uterus

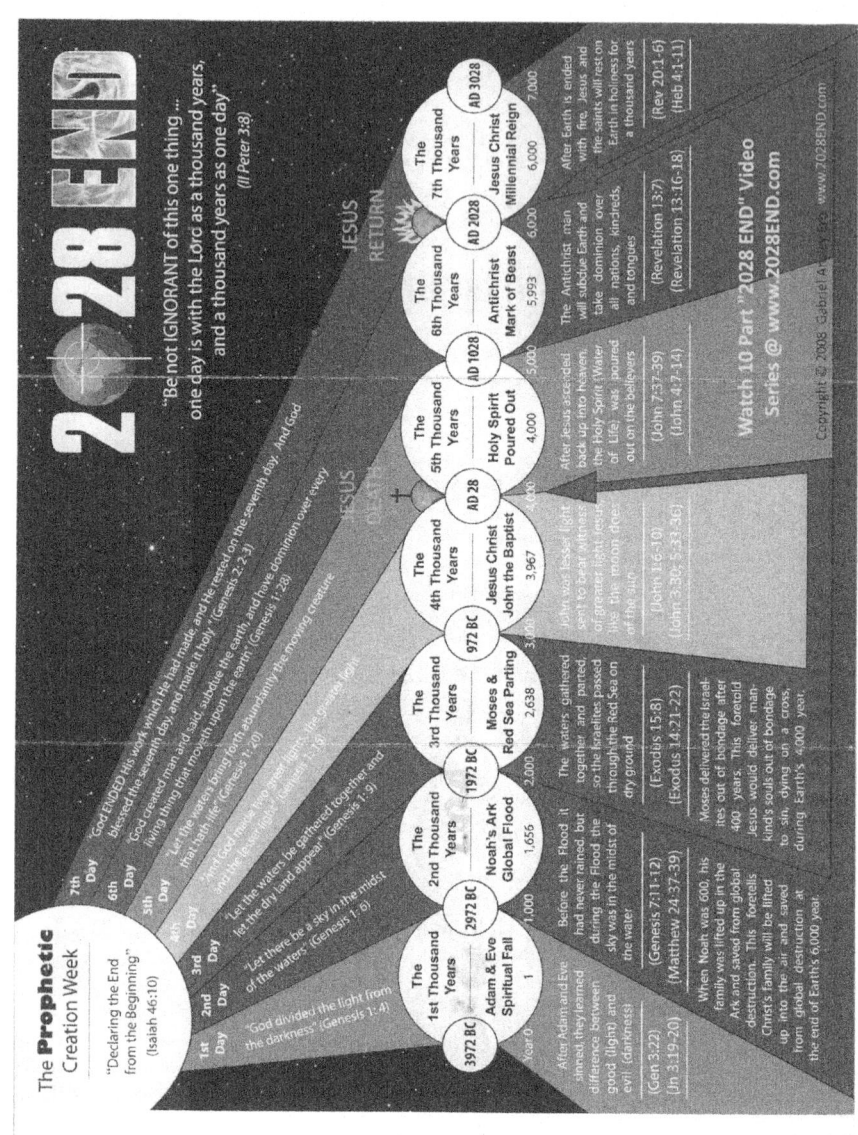

The **Prophetic** Creation Week

"Declaring the End from the Beginning" (Isaiah 46:10)

"Be not IGNORANT of this one thing ... one day is with the LORD as a thousand years, and a thousand years as one day." (II Peter 3:8)

JESUS RETURN

JESUS DEATH

	The 1st Thousand Years	The 2nd Thousand Years	The 3rd Thousand Years	The 4th Thousand Years	The 5th Thousand Years	The 6th Thousand Years	The 7th Thousand Years
	3972 BC	2972 BC	1972 BC	972 BC	AD 28	AD 1028	AD 2028	AD 3028
	Adam & Eve Spiritual Fall	Noah's Ark Global Flood	Moses & Red Sea Parting	Jesus Christ John the Baptist	Holy Spirit Poured Out	Antichrist Mark of Beast	Jesus Christ Millennial Reign

7th Day — "God ENDED His work which He had made and He rested on the seventh day; And God blessed the seventh day, and made it holy." (Genesis 2:1-3)

6th Day — "God created man and said, subdue the earth, and have dominion over every living thing that moveth upon the earth" (Genesis 1:26)

5th Day — "Let the waters bring forth abundantly the moving creature that hath life" (Genesis 1:20)

4th Day — "and God made two great lights; the greater light to rule the day" (Genesis 1:16)

3rd Day — "Let the waters be gathered together and let the dry land appear" (Genesis 1:9)

2nd Day — "Let there be a sky in the midst of the waters" (Genesis 1:6)

1st Day — "God divided the light from the darkness" (Genesis 1:4)

Year 0
1
1,000
2,000
3,967

After Adam and Eve sinned, they learned difference between good (light) and evil (darkness)

(Gen 3:22)
(Jn 3:19-20)

When Noah was 600, his family was lifted up in the Ark and saved from global destruction. This foretells Christ's family will be lifted up into the air and saved from global destruction at the end of Earth's 6,000 year.

Before the Flood it had never rained, but during the Flood the sky was in the midst of the water.

(Genesis 7:11-12)
(Matthew 24:37-39)

The waters gathered together and parted so the Israelites passed through the Red Sea on dry ground.

(Exodus 15:8)
(Exodus 14:21-22)

Moses delivered the Israelites out of bondage after 400 years. This foretold Jesus would deliver mankind's souls out of bondage to sin, dying on a cross, during Earth's 4,000 year.

John was lesser light sent to bear witness of greater light Jesus like the moon does of the sun.

(John 1:6-10)
(John 3:30; 5:33-36)

After Jesus ascended back up into Heaven the Holy Spirit (Water of Life) was poured out on the believers

(John 7:37-39)
(John 4:7-14)

The Antichrist man will subdue Earth and take dominion over all nations, kindreds, and tongues

(Revelation 13:7)
(Revelation 13:16-18)

After Earth is ended with fire, Jesus and the saints will rest on Earth in holiness for a thousand years

(Rev 20:1-6)
(Heb 4:1-11)

2,638
1,656
3,967
2,000
3,000
4,000
5,000
6,000
7,000

Watch 10 Part "2028 END" Video Series @ www.2028END.com

Copyright © 2008 Gabriel Ansley Erb   www.2028END.com

224

Made in the USA
Monee, IL
11 May 2021